Acclaim for EDWARD W. SAID's

Representations of the Intellectual

"Edward Said defines a corrective way to think about politics, drawing an urgent and absolutely necessary line between individual responsibility and the authority of consensus."

—*Joan Didion*

"Edward Said is that rare sort of intellectual who is able to illuminate even the stormiest of human prospects with a serene, often revelatory light that shows us not only the obligatory two sides to every question, but the often overlooked third dimension as well."

—*Gore Vidal*

"Said, one of our leading literary critics, is a rare example of an American academic who is also an intellectual in the European sense."

—*Camille Paglia*

"Courage, independence of mind, scholarship, compassion for the oppressed. . . . Absent though these qualities may be from our 'official' intellectuals, they are present in force in the person and works of Edward Said."

—*Alexander Cockburn*

Also by EDWARD W. SAID

EDWARD W. SAID

Representations
of the Intellectual

An internationally renowned literary and cultural
critic, Edward W. Said is University Professor at
Columbia University. He is the author of fourteen
other books, including *Orientalism*, which was nomi-
nated for the National Book Critics Circle Award,
Culture and Imperialism, *The Politics of Dispossession*,
and, most recently, *Peace and Its Discontents*.

Representations of the Intellectual

THE 1993 REITH LECTURES

Edward W. Said

VINTAGE BOOKS

A DIVISION OF RANDOM HOUSE, INC.

NEW YORK

First Vintage Books Edition, April 1996

The Library of Congress has cataloged the Pantheon edition
as follows:
Said, Edward W.
Representations of the intellectual : the Reith lectures /
Edward W. Said.
p. cm.
ISBN 0-679-43586-7
1. Intellectuals. 2. Intellectuals in literature. I. Title.
II. Title: Reith lectures.
HM213.S225 1994
305.5'52—dc20 94-3950
CIP
Vintage ISBN: 0-679-76127-6

Book design by Fearn Cutler

Printed in the United States of America
4 6 8 9 7 5 3

For Ben Sonnenberg

CONTENTS

INTRODUCTION

THERE IS NO equivalent for the Reith Lectures in the United States, although several Americans, Robert Oppenheimer, John Kenneth Galbraith, John Searle, have delivered them since the series was inaugurated in 1948 by Bertrand Russell. I had heard some of them over the air— I particularly remember Toynbee's series in 1950—as a boy growing up in the Arab world, where the BBC was a very important part of our life; even today phrases like "London said this morning" are a common refrain in the Middle East. They are always used with the assumption that "London" tells the truth. Whether this view of the BBC is only a vestige of colonialism I cannot tell, yet it is also true that in England and abroad the BBC has a position in public life enjoyed neither by government agencies like the Voice of America nor by the American networks, including CNN. One reason is that programs like the Reith Lectures and the many discussion and documentary shows are presented by the BBC, not so much as officially sanctioned programs, but as occasions that offer listeners and viewers an impressive range of serious, often distinguished material.

I was therefore very honored to be offered the opportunity by Anne Winder of the BBC to give the 1993 Reith Lectures. Because of scheduling problems we agreed on a date in late June rather than the customary January time slot. But almost from the moment that the announcement of the lectures was made by the BBC in late 1992 there was a persistent, albeit relatively small chorus of criticism directed at it for having invited me in the first place. I was accused of being active in the battle for Palestinian rights, and thus disqualified for any sober or respectable platform at all. This was only the first in a series of plainly anti-intellectual and antirational arguments, all of them ironically supporting the thesis of my lectures about the public role of the intellectual as outsider, "amateur," and disturber of the status quo.

These criticisms do in fact reveal a great deal about British attitudes to the intellectual. Of course these are attitudes imputed to the British public by journalists, but the frequency of their repetition gives these notions some current social credibility. Commenting on the announced themes of my Reith Lectures—Representations of the Intellectual—a sympathetic journalist states that it was a most "un-English" thing to talk about. Associated with the word "intellectual" was "ivory tower" and "a sneer." This depressing train of thought is underlined by the late Raymond Williams in *Keywords*. "Until the middle twentieth century unfavourable uses of *intellectuals, intellectualism* and *intel-*

ligentsia were dominant in English," he says, "and it is clear that such uses persist."[1]

One task of the intellectual is the effort to break down the stereotypes and reductive categories that are so limiting to human thought and communication. I had no idea of the limitations to which I was subject, before I gave the lectures. It was often said by complaining journalists and commentators that I was a Palestinian, and that, as everyone knew, was synonymous with violence, fanaticism, the killing of Jews. Nothing by me was quoted: it was just supposed to be a matter of common knowledge. In addition, I was described in the sonorous tones of *The Sunday Telegraph* as anti-Western, and my writing as focused on "blaming the West" for all the evils of the world, the Third World especially.

What seemed to have completely escaped notice was everything I had actually written in a whole series of books, including *Orientalism* and *Culture and Imperialism*. (My unforgivable sin in the latter is my argument that Jane Austen's *Mansfield Park*—a novel I praise as much as I do all her work—also had something to do with slavery and British-owned sugar plantations in Antigua, both of which of course she mentions quite specifically. My point was that just as Austen talks about goings-on in Britain and in British overseas possessions, so too must her twentieth-century reader and critics, who have for too long focused on the former to the exclusion of the latter.) The construc-

---

[1]Raymond Williams, *Keywords: A Vocabulary of Culture and Society* (1976; rprt. New York: Oxford University Press, 1985), p. 170.

tion of fictions like "East" and "West," to say nothing of racialist essences like subject races, Orientals, Aryans, Negroes and the like, were what my books attempted to combat. Far from encouraging a sense of aggrieved primal innocence in countries which had suffered the ravages of colonialism, I stated repeatedly that mythical abstractions such as these were lies, as were the various rhetorics of blame they gave rise to; cultures are too intermingled, their contents and histories too interdependent and hybrid, for surgical separation into large and mostly ideological oppositions like Orient and Occident.

Even well-meaning critics of my Reith Lectures—commentators who seemed to have a real acquaintance with what I said—assumed that my claims for the intellectual's role in society contained a veiled autobiographical message. What about right-wing intellectuals like Wyndham Lewis or William Buckley, I was asked. Why, according to you, must every intellectual be a man or woman of the Left? What was not noticed was the fact that Julien Benda, whom I rely on (perhaps paradoxically) with some frequency, was very much of the Right. In fact, the attempt in these lectures is rather to speak about intellectuals as precisely those figures whose public performances can neither be predicted nor compelled into some slogan, orthodox party line, or fixed dogma. What I was trying to suggest was that standards of truth about human misery and oppression were to be held to despite the individual intellectual's party affiliation, national background, and primeval loyalties. Nothing disfigures the intellectual's public performance as much as trimming, careful silence, patriotic bluster, and retrospective and self-dramatizing apostasy.

The attempt to hold to a universal and single standard as a theme plays an important role in my account of the intellectual. Or rather the interaction between universality and the local, the subjective, the here and now. John Carey's interesting book *The Intellectuals and the Masses: Pride and Prejudice Among the Literary Intelligentsia 1880–1939*[2] appeared in America after I had written my lectures, but I found its on the whole dispiriting findings complementary to mine. According to Carey, British intellectuals like Gissing, Wells, and Wyndham Lewis detested the rise of modern mass societies, lamenting such things as "the common man," suburbia, middle-class taste; instead they promoted a natural aristocracy, "better" earlier times, high-class culture. For me the intellectual appeals to (rather than excoriates) as wide as possible a public, who is his or her natural constituency. The problem for the intellectual is not so much, as Carey discusses, mass society as a whole, but rather the insiders, experts, coteries, professionals who in the modes defined earlier this century by pundit Walter Lippmann mold public opinion, make it conformist, encourage a reliance on a superior little band of all-knowing men in power. Insiders promote special interests, but intellectuals should be the ones to question patriotic nationalism, corporate thinking, and a sense of class, racial or gender privilege.

[2]John Carey, *The Intellectuals and the Masses: Pride and Prejudice Among the Literary Intelligentsia 1880–1939* (New York: St Martin's Press, 1993).

Universality means taking a risk in order to go beyond the easy certainties provided us by our background, language, nationality, which so often shield us from the reality of others. It also means looking for and trying to uphold a single standard for human behavior when it comes to such matters as foreign and social policy. Thus if we condemn an unprovoked act of aggression by an enemy we should also be able to do the same when our government invades a weaker party. There are no rules by which intellectuals can know what to say or do; nor for the true secular intellectual are there any gods to be worshiped and looked to for unwavering guidance.

In such circumstances the social terrain is not only diverse, but very difficult to negotiate. Thus Ernest Gellner in an essay entitled "La trahison de la trahison des clercs," which upbraids Benda's uncritical platonism, ends up leaving us exactly nowhere, less clear than Benda, less courageous than the Sartre he criticizes, less useful even than some who claimed to be following a crude dogma: "What I *am* saying is that the task of *not* committing [*la trahison des clercs*] is far, far more difficult than an appallingly simplified model of the intellectual's work situation would have us believe."[3] Gellner's vacuous caution, very much like Paul Johnson's scurrilous, as well as hopelessly cynical, attack on all intellectuals ("a dozen people picked at random on the street are at least as likely to offer sensible

---

[3]Ernest Gellner, "La trahison de la trahison des clercs," in *The Political Responsibility of Intellectuals,* eds. Ian Maclean, Alan Montefiore and Peter Winch (Cambridge: Cambridge University Press, 1990), p. 27.

views on moral and political matters as a cross-section of the intelligentsia"[4]), leads to the conclusion that there can be no such thing as an intellectual vocation, an absence to be celebrated.

I disagree, not only because a coherent description for that vocation can be provided, but also because the world is more crowded than it ever has been with professionals, experts, consultants, in a word, with *intellectuals* whose main role is to provide authority with their labor while gaining great profit. There are a set of concrete choices facing the intellectual, and it is these that I characterize in my lectures. First of course is the notion that all intellectuals represent something to their audiences, and in so doing represent themselves to themselves. Whether you are an academic, or a bohemian essayist, or a consultant to the Defense Department, you do what you do according to an idea or representation you have of yourself as doing that thing: do you think of yourself as providing "objective" advice for pay, or do you believe that what you teach your students has truth value, or do you think of yourself as a personality advocating an eccentric but consistent perspective?

All of us live in a society, and are members of a nationality with its own language, tradition, historical situation. To what extent are intellectuals servants of these actualities, to what extent enemies? The same is true of intellectuals' relationship with institutions (academy,

---

[4]Paul Johnson, *Intellectuals* (London: Weidenfeld and Nicholson, 1988), p. 342.

church, professional guild) and with worldly powers, which in our time have co-opted the intelligentsia to an extraordinary degree. The results are, as Wilfred Owen put it, that "the scribes on all the people shove/And bawl allegiance to the state." Thus in my view the principal intellectual duty is the search for relative independence from such pressures. Hence my characterizations of the intellectual as exile and marginal, as amateur, and as the author of a language that tries to speak the truth to power.

One of the virtues, as well as the difficulties, of actually giving the Reith Lectures is that you are constrained by the inflexible rigor of the thirty-minute broadcast format: one lecture a week for six weeks. Yet you do directly address a huge live audience, much bigger than intellectuals and academics normally lecture to. For a subject as complex and potentially endless as mine, this laid a special burden on me to be as precise, accessible and economical as possible. In preparing them for publication I kept them pretty much as I gave them, adding only an occasional reference or example, the better to preserve both the immediacy and required conciseness of the original, with no real opportunities left in the text for fudging, or otherwise diluting or qualifying my main points.

So while I have little to add that would change the ideas set forth here, I should like this introduction to supply just a little more context. In underlining the intellectual's role as outsider I have had in mind how powerless one often feels in the face of an overwhelmingly powerful network of social authorities—the media, the government

and corporations, etc.—who crowd out the possibilities
for achieving any change. To deliberately not belong to
these authorities is in many ways not to be able to effect
direct change and, alas, even at times to be relegated to
the role of a witness who testifies to a horror otherwise
unrecorded. A very moving recent account of the gifted
African-American essayist and novelist James Baldwin
by Peter Dailey particularly well renders this condition
of being a "witness" in all its pathos and ambiguous
eloquence.[5]

But there can be little doubt that figures like Baldwin
and Malcolm X define the kind of work that has most
influenced my own representations of the intellectual's
consciousness. It is a spirit in opposition, rather than in
accommodation, that grips me because the romance, the
interest, the challenge of intellectual life is to be found in
dissent against the status quo at a time when the struggle
on behalf of underrepresented and disadvantaged groups
seems so unfairly weighted against them. My background
in Palestinian politics has further intensified this sense.
Both in the West and the Arab world the fissure separating
haves and have-nots deepens every day, and among intellectuals in power it brings out smug heedlessness that is
truly appalling. What could be less attractive and less true
a couple of years after it was all the rage than Fukuyama's
"end of history" thesis or Lyotard's account of the "disappearance" of the "grand narratives"? The same can be

[5]Peter Dailey, "Jimmy," *The American Scholar* (Winter 1994), 102–10.

said of the hardheaded pragmatists and realists who concocted preposterous fictions like the New World Order or "the clash of civilizations."

I do not want to be misunderstood. Intellectuals are not required to be humorless complainers. Nothing less could be true of such celebrated and energetic dissenters as Noam Chomsky or Gore Vidal. Witnessing a sorry state of affairs when one is not in power is by no means a monotonous, monochromatic activity. It involves what Foucault once called "a relentless erudition," scouring alternative sources, exhuming buried documents, reviving forgotten (or abandoned) histories. It involves a sense of the dramatic and of the insurgent, making a great deal of one's rare opportunities to speak, catching the audience's attention, being better at wit and debate than one's opponents. And there is something fundamentally unsettling about intellectuals who have neither offices to protect nor territory to consolidate and guard; self-irony is therefore more frequent than pomposity, directness more than hemming and hawing. But there is no dodging the inescapable reality that such representations by intellectuals will neither make them friends in high places nor win them official honors. It is a lonely condition, yes, but it is always a better one than a gregarious tolerance for the way things are.

I am greatly indebted to Anne Winder of the BBC and her assistant Sarah Ferguson. As the producer in charge of these lectures Ms. Winder guided me wittily and wisely through the process. Whatever flaws remain are of course entirely my own. Frances Coady edited the manuscript with tact and intelligence. I am most grateful to her. In New York, Shelley Wanger of Pantheon graciously helped me through the editorial march. To her, many thanks. For their interest in these lectures and graciousness in publishing extracts from them I am also grateful to my dear friends Richard Poirier, editor of *Raritan Review,* and Jean Stein, editor of *Grand Street.* The substance of these pages was constantly illuminated and invigorated by the example of many fine intellectuals and good friends, a list of whose names here would perhaps be embarrassing for them and might seem invidious. Some of their names appear in the lectures themselves in any case. I salute them and thank them for their solidarity and instruction. Dr. Zaineb Istrabadi helped me in all phases of preparing these lectures: for her able assistance I am very thankful.

E.W.S.
New York
February 1994

Representations of the Intellectual

Representations of the Intellectual

I

Representations of the Intellectual

ARE INTELLECTUALS a very large or an extremely small and highly selective group of people? Two of the most famous twentieth-century descriptions of intellectuals are fundamentally opposed on that point. Antonio Gramsci, the Italian Marxist, activist, journalist and brilliant political philosopher who was imprisoned by Mussolini between 1926 and 1937, wrote in his *Prison Notebooks* that "all men are intellectuals, one could therefore say: but not all men have in society the function of intellectuals."[1] Gramsci's own career exemplifies the role he ascribed to the intellectual: a trained philologist, he was both an organizer of the Italian working-class movement and, in his own journalism, one of the most consciously reflective of social analysts, whose purpose was to build not just a social move-

[1]Antonio Gramsci, *The Prison Notebooks: Selections,* trans. Quintin Hoare and Geoffrey Nowell-Smith (New York: International Publishers, 1971), p. 9.

3

ment but an entire cultural formation associated with the movement.

Those who do perform the intellectual function in society, Gramsci tries to show, can be divided into two types: first, traditional intellectuals such as teachers, priests, and administrators, who continue to do the same thing from generation to generation; and second, organic intellectuals, whom Gramsci saw as directly connected to classes or enterprises that used intellectuals to organize interests, gain more power, get more control. Thus, Gramsci says about the organic intellectual, "the capitalist entrepreneur creates alongside himself the industrial technician, the specialist in political economy, the organizers of a new culture, of a new legal system, etc."[2] Today's advertising or public relations expert, who devises techniques for winning a detergent or airline company a larger share of the market, would be considered an organic intellectual according to Gramsci, someone who in a democratic society tries to gain the consent of potential customers, win approval, marshal consumer or voter opinion. Gramsci believed that organic intellectuals are actively involved in society, that is, they constantly struggle to change minds and expand markets; unlike teachers and priests, who seem more or less to remain in place, doing the same kind of work year in year out, organic intellectuals are always on the move, on the make.

At the other extreme there is Julien Benda's celebrated definition of intellectuals as a tiny band of super-

[2] Ibid., p. 4.

gifted and morally endowed philosopher-kings who constitute the conscience of mankind. While it is true that Benda's treatise *La trahison des clercs*—The betrayal of the intellectuals—has lived in posterity more as a blistering attack on intellectuals who abandon their calling and compromise their principles than as a systematic analysis of intellectual life, he does in fact cite a small number of names and major characteristics of those whom he considered to be real intellectuals. Socrates and Jesus are frequently mentioned, as are more recent exemplars like Spinoza, Voltaire and Ernest Renan. Real intellectuals constitute a clerisy, very rare creatures indeed, since what they uphold are eternal standards of truth and justice that are precisely *not* of this world. Hence Benda's religious term for them—clerics—a distinction in status and performance that he always counterposes against the laity, those ordinary human beings who are interested in material advantage, personal advancement, and, if at all possible, a close relationship with secular powers. Real intellectuals, he says, are "those whose activity is essentially not the pursuit of practical aims, all those who seek their joy in the practice of an art or a science or metaphysical speculation, in short in the possession of non-material advantages, and hence in a certain manner say: 'My kingdom is not of this world.' "[3]

Benda's examples, however, make it quite clear that he does not endorse the notion of totally disengaged, other

[3]Julien Benda, *The Treason of the Intellectuals*, trans. Richard Aldington (1928; rprt. New York: Norton, 1969), p. 43.

worldly, ivory-towered thinkers, intensely private and devoted to abstruse, perhaps even occult subjects. Real intellectuals are never more themselves than when, moved
by metaphysical passion and disinterested principles of justice and truth, they denounce corruption, defend the weak,
defy imperfect or oppressive authority. "Need I recall,"
he says, "how Fenelon and Massillon denounced certain
wars of Louis XIV? How Voltaire condemned the destruction of the Palatinate? How Renan denounced the vio-
lences of Napoleon? Buckle, the intolerances of England
toward the French Revolution? And, in our times,
Nietzsche, the brutalities of Germany towards France?"[4]
The trouble with today's lot according to Benda is that
they have conceded their moral authority to what, in a
prescient phrase, he calls "the organization of collective
passions" such as sectarianism, mass sentiment, nationalist
belligerence, class interests. Benda was writing in 1927,
well before the age of the mass media, but he sensed how
important it was for governments to have as their servants
those intellectuals who could be called on not to lead, but
to consolidate the government's policy, to spew out prop-
aganda against official enemies, euphemisms and, on a
larger scale, whole systems of Orwellian Newspeak, which
could disguise the truth of what was occurring in the name
of institutional "expediency" or "national honor."

The force of Benda's jeremiad against the betrayal of
the intellectuals is not the subtlety of his argument, nor
his quite impossible absolutism when it comes to his totally

[4] Ibid., p. 52.

uncompromising view of the intellectual's mission. Real intellectuals, according to Benda's definition, are supposed to risk being burned at the stake, ostracized, or crucified. They are symbolic personages marked by their unyielding distance from practical concerns. As such therefore they cannot be many in number, nor routinely developed. They have to be thoroughgoing individuals with powerful personalities and, above all, they have to be in a state of almost permanent opposition to the status quo: for all these reasons Benda's intellectuals are inevitably a small, highly visible group of men—he never includes women—whose stentorian voices and indelicate imprecations are hurled at humankind from on high. Benda never suggests how it is that these men know the truth, or whether their blinding insights into eternal principles might, like those of Don Quixote, be little more than private fantasies.

But there is no doubt in my mind at least that the image of a real intellectual as generally conceived by Benda remains an attractive and compelling one. Many of his positive, as well as negative, examples are persuasive: Voltaire's public defense of the Calas family, for instance, or—at the opposite end—the appalling nationalism of French writers like Maurice Barrès, whom Benda credits with perpetuating a "romanticism of harshness and contempt" in the name of French national honor.[5] Benda was spiritually

[5]In 1762 a Protestant merchant, Jean Calas of Toulouse, was judged, then executed for the alleged murder of his son, about to convert to Catholicism. The evidence was flimsy, yet what produced the speedy verdict was the widespread belief that Protestants were fanatics who simply did away with any other Protestant who wanted to convert. Voltaire led a

shaped by the Dreyfus Affair and World War One, both of them rigorous tests for intellectuals, who could either choose to speak up courageously against an act of anti-Semitic military injustice and nationalist fervor, or sheepishly go along with the herd, refusing to defend the unfairly condemned Jewish officer Alfred Dreyfus, chanting jingoist slogans in order to stir up war fever against everything German. After World War Two Benda republished his book, this time adding a series of attacks against intellectuals who collaborated with the Nazis as well as against those who were uncritically enthusiastic about the Communists.[6] But deep in the combative rhetoric of Benda's basically very conservative work is to be found this figure of the intellectual as a being set apart, someone able to speak the truth to power, a crusty, eloquent, fantastically courageous and angry individual for whom no worldly power is too big and imposing to be criticized and pointedly taken to task.

Gramsci's social analysis of the intellectual as a person who fulfills a particular set of functions in the society is much closer to the reality than anything Benda gives us, particularly in the late twentieth century when so many new professions—broadcasters, academic professionals,

---

successful public campaign to rehabilitate the Calas family's reputation (yet we now know that he too manufactured his own evidence). Maurice Barrès was a prominent opponent of Alfred Dreyfus. A proto-fascist and anti-intellectual late-nineteenth- and early-twentieth-century French novelist, he advocated a notion of the political unconscious, in which whole races and nations carried ideas and tendencies collectively.

[6]*La Trahison* was republished by Bernard Grasset in 1946.

computer analysts, sports and media lawyers, management consultants, policy experts, government advisers, authors of specialized market reports, and indeed the whole field of modern mass journalism itself—have vindicated Gramsci's vision.

Today, everyone who works in any field connected either with the production or distribution of knowledge is an intellectual in Gramsci's sense. In most industrialized Western societies the ratio between so-called knowledge industries and those having to do with actual physical production has increased steeply in favor of the knowledge industries. The American sociologist Alvin Gouldner said several years ago of intellectuals that they were the new class, and that intellectual managers had now pretty much replaced the old monied and propertied classes. Yet Gouldner also said that as part of their ascendancy intellectuals were no longer people who addressed a wide public; instead they had become members of what he called a culture of critical discourse.[7] Each intellectual, the book editor and the author, the military strategist and the international lawyer, speaks and deals in a language that has become specialized and usable by other members of the same field, specialized experts addressing other specialized experts in a *lingua franca* largely unintelligible to unspecialized people.

Similarly, the French philosopher Michel Foucault has said that the so-called universal intellectual (he probably

[7]Alvin W. Gouldner, *The Future of Intellectuals and the Rise of the New Class* (New York: Seabury Press, 1979), pp. 28–43.

had Jean-Paul Sartre in mind) has had his or her place taken by the "specific" intellectual,[8] someone who works inside a discipline but who is able to use his expertise anyway. Here Foucault was thinking specifically of American physicist Robert Oppenheimer, who moved outside his specialist field when he was an organizer of the Los Alamos atomic bomb project in 1942–45 and later became a sort of commissar of scientific affairs in the U.S.

And the proliferation of intellectuals has extended even into the very large number of fields in which intellectuals—possibly following on Gramsci's pioneering suggestions in *The Prison Notebooks* which almost for the first time saw intellectuals, and not social classes, as pivotal to the workings of modern society—have become the object of study. Just put the words "of" and "and" next to the word "intellectuals" and almost immediately an entire library of studies about intellectuals that is quite daunting in its range and minutely focused in its detail rises before our eyes. There are thousands of different histories and sociologies of intellectuals available, as well as endless accounts of intellectuals and nationalism, and power, and tradition, and revolution, and on and on. Each region of the world has produced its intellectuals and each of those formations is debated and argued over with fiery passion. There has been no major revolution in modern history

[8]Michel Foucault, *Power/Knowledge: Selected Interviews and Other Writings 1972–1977*, ed. Colin Gordon (New York: Pantheon, 1980), pp. 127–28.

without intellectuals; conversely there has been no major counterrevolutionary movement without intellectuals. Intellectuals have been the fathers and mothers of movements, and of course sons and daughters, even nephews and nieces.

There is a danger that the figure or image of the intellectual might disappear in a mass of details, and that the intellectual might become only another professional or a figure in a social trend. What I shall be arguing in these lectures takes for granted these late-twentieth-century realities originally suggested by Gramsci, but I also want to insist that the intellectual is an individual with a specific public role in society that cannot be reduced simply to being a faceless professional, a competent member of a class just going about her/his business. The central fact for me is, I think, that the intellectual is an individual endowed with a faculty for representing, embodying, articulating a message, a view, an attitude, philosophy or opinion to, as well as for, a public. And this role has an edge to it, and cannot be played without a sense of being someone whose place it is publicly to raise embarrassing questions, to confront orthodoxy and dogma (rather than to produce them), to be someone who cannot easily be co-opted by governments or corporations, and whose *raison d'être* is to represent all those people and issues that are routinely forgotten or swept under the rug. The intellectual does so on the basis of universal principles: that all human beings are entitled to expect decent standards of behavior concerning freedom and justice from worldly powers or nations, and that deliberate or inadvertent violations of these standards need to be testified and fought against courageously.

Let me put this in personal terms: as an intellectual I present my concerns before an audience or constituency, but this is not just a matter of how I articulate them, but also of what I myself, as someone who is trying to advance the cause of freedom and justice, also represent. I say or write these things because after much reflection they are what I believe; and I also want to persuade others of this view. There is therefore this quite complicated mix between the private and the public worlds, my own history, values, writings and positions as they derive from my experiences, on the one hand, and, on the other hand, how these enter into the social world where people debate and make decisions about war and freedom and justice. There is no such thing as a private intellectual, since the moment you set down words and then publish them you have entered the public world. Nor is there *only* a public intellectual, someone who exists just as a figurehead or spokesperson or symbol of a cause, movement, or position. There is always the personal inflection and the private sensibility, and those give meaning to what is being said or written. Least of all should an intellectual be there to make his/her audiences feel good: the whole point is to be embarrassing, contrary, even unpleasant.

So in the end it is the intellectual as a representative figure that matters—someone who visibly represents a standpoint of some kind, and someone who makes articulate representations to his or her public despite all sorts of barriers. My argument is that intellectuals are individuals with a vocation for the art of representing, whether that is talking, writing, teaching, appearing on television. And that vocation is important to the extent that it is publicly recognizable and involves both commitment and risk, boldness and vulnerability; when I read Jean-Paul Sartre or Bertrand Russell it is their specific, individual voice and presence that makes an impression on me over and above their arguments because they are speaking out for their beliefs. They cannot be mistaken for an anonymous functionary or careful bureaucrat.

In the outpouring of studies about intellectuals there has been far too much defining of the intellectual, and not enough stock taken of the image, the signature, the actual intervention and performance, all of which taken together constitute the very lifeblood of every real intellectual. Isaiah Berlin has said of nineteenth-century Russian writers that, partly under the influence of German romanticism, their audiences were "made conscious that he was on a public stage, testifying."[9] Something of that quality still adheres to the public role of the modern intellectual as I see it. That is why when we remember an intellectual like Sartre we recall the personal mannerisms, the sense of an important personal stake, the sheer effort, risk, will to say things about colonialism, or about commitment, or about social conflict that infuriated his opponents and galvanized his friends and perhaps even embarrassed him retrospectively. When we read about Sartre's involvement

[9]Isaiah Berlin, *Russian Thinkers,* ed. Henry Hardy and Aileen Kelly (New York: Viking Press, 1978), p. 129.

with Simone de Beauvoir, his dispute with Camus, his remarkable association with Jean Genet, we situate him (the word is Sartre's) in his circumstances; in these circumstances, and to some extent because of them, Sartre was Sartre, the same person who also opposed France in Algeria and Vietnam. Far from disabling or disqualifying him as an intellectual, these complications give texture and tension to what he said, expose him as a fallible human being, not a dreary and moralistic preacher.

It is in modern public life seen as a novel or drama and not as a business or as the raw material for a sociological monograph that we can most readily see and understand how it is that intellectuals are representative, not just of some subterranean or large social movement, but of a quite peculiar, even abrasive style of life and social performance that is uniquely theirs. And where better to find that role first described than in certain unusual nineteenth- and early-twentieth-century novels—Turgenev's *Fathers and Sons,* Flaubert's *Sentimental Education,* Joyce's *A Portrait of the Artist as a Young Man*—in which the representation of social reality is profoundly influenced, even decisively changed by the sudden appearance of a new actor, the modern young intellectual.

Turgenev's portrait of provincial Russia in the 1860s is idyllic and uneventful: young men of property inherit their habits of life from their parents, they marry and have children, and life more or less moves on. This is the case until an anarchic and yet highly concentrated figure, Bazarov, erupts into their lives. The first thing we notice about him is that he has severed his ties with his own parents, and seems less a son than a sort of self-produced character, challenging routine, assailing mediocrity and clichés, asserting new scientific and unsentimental values that appear to be rational and progressive. Turgenev said that he refused to dip Bazarov in syrup; he was meant to be "coarse, heartless, ruthlessly dry and brusque." Bazarov makes fun of the Kirsanov family; when the middle-aged father plays Schubert, Bazarov laughs loudly at him. Bazarov propounds the ideas of German materialist science: nature for him is not a temple, it is a workshop. When he falls in love with Anna Sergeyevna she is attracted to him, but also terrified: to her, his untrammeled, often anarchical intellectual energy suggests chaos. Being with him, she says at one point, is like teetering at the edge of an abyss.

The beauty and pathos of the novel is that Turgenev suggests, and portrays, the incompatibility between a Russia governed by families, the continuities of love and filial affection, the old natural way of doing things, and at the same time, the nihilistically disruptive force of a Bazarov, whose history, unlike that of every other character in the novel, seems to be impossible to narrate. He appears, he challenges, and just as abruptly, he dies, infected by a sick peasant whom he had been treating. What we remember of Bazarov is the sheer unremitting force of his quest and deeply confrontational intellect; and although Turgenev claimed to have believed he was his most sympathetic character, even he was mystified and to some extent stopped by Bazarov's heedless intellectual force, as well as by his readers' quite bewilderingly turbulent reactions. Some readers thought that Bazarov was an attack on youth; others praised the character as a true hero; still others thought him dangerous. Whatever we may feel about him as a person, *Fathers and Sons* cannot accommodate Bazarov as a character in the narrative; whereas his friends the Kirsanov family, and even his pathetic old parents, go on with their lives, his peremptoriness and defiance as an intellectual lift him out of the story, unsuited to it and somehow not fit for domestication.

This is even more explicitly the case with Joyce's young Stephen Dedalus, whose entire early career is a seesaw between the blandishments of institutions like the church, the profession of teaching, Irish nationalism, and his slowly emerging and stubborn selfhood as an intellectual whose motto is the Luciferian *non serviam*. Seamus Deane makes an excellent observation about Joyce's *Portrait of the Artist:* it is, he says, "the first novel in the English language in which a passion for thinking is fully presented."[10] Neither the protagonists of Dickens, nor Thackeray, nor Austen, nor Hardy, nor even George Eliot are young men and women whose major concern is the life of the mind in society, whereas for young Dedalus "thinking is a mode of experiencing the world." Deane is quite correct in saying that before Dedalus the intellectual vocation had only "grotesque embodiments" in English fiction. Yet in part because Stephen is a young provincial, the product of a colonial environment, he must develop a resistant intellectual consciousness before he can become an artist.

---

[10]Seamus Deane, *Celtic Revivals: Essays in Modern Irish Literature 1880–1980* (London: Faber & Faber, 1985), pp. 75–76.

By the end of the novel he is no less critical and withdrawn from family and Fenians than he is from any ideological scheme whose effect would be to reduce his individuality and his often very unpleasant personality. Like Turgenev, Joyce pointedly enacts the incompatibility between the young intellectual and the sequential flow of human life. What begins as a conventional story of a young man growing up in a family, then moving on to school and university, decomposes into a series of elliptical jottings from Stephen's notebook. The intellectual will not adjust to domesticity or to humdrum routine. In the novel's most famous speech Stephen expresses what is in effect the intellectual's creed of freedom, although the melodramatic overstatement in Stephen's declaration is Joyce's way of undercutting the young man's pomposity: "I will tell you what I will do and what I will not do. I will not serve that in which I no longer believe whether it call itself my home, my fatherland or my church: and I will try to express myself in some mode of life or art as freely as I can and as wholly as I can, using for my defence the only arms I allow myself to use—silence, exile, and cunning."

Yet not even in *Ulysses* do we see Stephen as more than an obstinate and contrary young man. What is most striking in his credo is his affirmation of intellectual freedom. This is a major issue in the intellectual's performance since being a curmudgeon and a thoroughgoing wet blanket are hardly enough as goals. The purpose of the intellectual's activity is to advance human freedom and knowledge. This is still true, I believe, despite the often repeated charge that "grand narratives of emancipation and enlightenment," as the contemporary French philosopher Lyotard calls such heroic ambitions associated with the previous "modern" age, are pronounced as no longer having any currency in the era of postmodernism. According to this view grand narratives have been replaced by local situations and language games; postmodern intellectuals now prize competence, not universal values like truth or freedom. I've always thought that Lyotard and his followers are admitting their own lazy incapacities, perhaps even indifference, rather than giving a correct assessment of what remains for the intellectual a truly vast array of opportunities despite postmodernism. For in fact governments still manifestly oppress people, grave miscarriages of justice still occur, the co-optation and inclusion of intellectuals by power can still effectively quieten their voices, and the deviation of intellectuals from their vocation is still very often the case.

In *The Sentimental Education* Flaubert expresses more disappointment with, and therefore a more merciless critique of, intellectuals than anyone. Set in the Parisian upheaval of 1848 to 1851, a period described by the famous British historian Lewis Namier as the revolution of the intellectuals, Flaubert's novel is a wide-ranging panorama of bohemian and political life in "the capital of the nineteenth century." At its center stand the two young provincials, Frédéric Moreau and Charles Deslauriers, whose exploits as young men-about-town express Flaubert's rage at their inability to maintain a steady course as intellectuals. Much of Flaubert's scorn for them comes from what is perhaps his exaggerated expectation of what they should have been. The result is the most brilliant representation of the intellectual adrift. The two young men start out as potential legal scholars, critics, historians, essayists, philosophers, and social theorists with public welfare as their goal. Moreau ends up "with his intellectual ambitions . . . dwindled. Years went by and he endured the idleness of his mind and the inertia of his heart." Deslauriers becomes "director of colonization in Algeria, secretary to a pasha, manager of a newspaper, and an advertising agent; . . . at present he was employed as solicitor to an industrial company."

The failures of 1848 are for Flaubert the failures of his generation. Prophetically, the fates of Moreau and Deslauriers are portrayed as the result of their own lack of focused will and also as the toll exacted by modern society, with its endless distractions, its whirl of pleasures, and, above all, the emergence of journalism, advertising, instant celebrity, and a sphere of constant circulation, in which all ideas are marketable, all values transmutable, all professions reduced to the pursuit of easy money and quick success. The novel's major scenes are therefore organized symbolically around horse races, dances at cafés and bordellos, riots, processions, parades, and public meetings, in which Moreau tries ceaselessly to achieve love and intellectual fulfillment, but is continually deflected from doing so.

Bazarov, Dedalus, and Moreau are extremes of course, but they do serve the purpose, which is something panoramic realistic novels of the nineteenth century can do uniquely well, of showing us intellectuals in action, beset with numerous difficulties and temptations, either maintaining or betraying their calling, not as a fixed task to be learned once and for all from a how-to-do-it manual but as a concrete experience constantly threatened by modern life itself. The intellectual's representations, his or her articulations of a cause or idea to society, are not meant primarily to fortify ego or celebrate status. Nor are they principally intended for service within powerful bureaucracies and with generous employers. Intellectual representations are the *activity itself,* dependent on a kind of consciousness that is skeptical, engaged, unremittingly devoted to rational investigation and moral judgment; and this puts the individual on record and on the line. Knowing how to use language well and knowing when to intervene in language are two essential features of intellectual action.

But what does the intellectual represent today? One of the best and most honest answers to this question was given, I think, by the American sociologist C. Wright Mills, a fiercely independent intellectual with an impassioned social vision and a remarkable capacity for communicating his ideas in a straightforward and compelling prose. He wrote in 1944 that independent intellectuals were faced either with a kind of despondent sense of powerlessness at their marginality, or with the choice of joining the ranks of institutions, corporations or governments as members of a relatively small group of insiders who made important decisions irresponsibly and on their own. To become the "hired" agent of an information industry is no solution either, since to achieve a relationship with audiences like Tom Paine's with his would therefore be impossible. In sum "the means of effective communication," which is the intellectual's currency, is thus being expropriated, leaving the independent thinker with one major task. Here is how Mills puts it:

> The independent artist and intellectual are among the few remaining personalities equipped to resist and to fight the stereotyping and consequent death of genuinely living things. Fresh perception now involves the capacity to continually unmask and to smash the stereotypes of vision and intellect with which modern communications [i.e. modern systems of representation] swamp us. These worlds of mass-art and mass-thought are increasingly geared to the demands of politics. That is why it is in politics that intellectual solidarity and effort must be centered. If the thinker does not relate himself to the value of truth in political struggle, he cannot responsibly cope with the whole of live experience.[11]

This passage deserves reading and rereading, so full of important signposts and emphases is it. Politics is everywhere; there can be no escape into the realms of pure art and thought or, for that matter, into the realm of disinterested objectivity or transcendental theory. Intellectuals are *of* their time, herded along by the mass politics of representations embodied by the information or media

[11]C. Wright Mills, *Power, Politics, and People: The Collected Essays of C. Wright Mills,* ed. Irving Louis Horowitz (New York: Ballantine, 1963), p. 299.

industry, capable of resisting those only by disputing the images, official narratives, justifications of power circulated by an increasingly powerful media—and not only media but whole trends of thought that maintain the status quo, keep things within an acceptable and sanctioned perspective on actuality—by providing what Mills calls unmaskings or alternative versions in which to the best of one's ability the intellectual tries to tell the truth.

This is far from an easy task: the intellectual always stands between loneliness and alignment. How difficult it was during the recent Gulf War against Iraq to remind citizens that the U.S. was not an innocent or disinterested power (the invasions of Vietnam and Panama were conveniently forgotten by policy-makers), nor was it appointed by anyone except itself as the world's policeman. But this was, I believe, the intellectuals' task at the time, to unearth the forgotten, to make connections that were denied, to cite alternative courses of action that could have avoided war and its attendant goal of human destruction.

C. Wright Mills's main point is the opposition between the mass and the individual. There is an inherent discrepancy between the powers of large organizations, from governments to corporations, and the relative weakness not just of individuals but of human beings considered to have subaltern status, minorities, small peoples and states, inferior or lesser cultures and races. There is no question in my mind that the intellectual belongs on the same side with the weak and unrepresented. Robin Hood, some are likely to say. Yet it's not that simple a role, and therefore cannot be easily dismissed as just so much romantic idealism. At bottom, the intellectual, in my sense of the word, is neither a pacifier nor a consensus-builder, but someone whose whole being is staked on a critical sense, a sense of being unwilling to accept easy formulas, or ready-made clichés, or the smooth, ever-so-accommodating confirmations of what the powerful or conventional have to say, and what they do. Not just passively unwillingly, but actively willing to say so in public.

This is not always a matter of being a critic of government policy, but rather of thinking of the intellectual vocation as maintaining a state of constant alertness, of a perpetual willingness not to let half-truths or received ideas steer one along. That this involves a steady realism, an almost athletic rational energy, and a complicated struggle to balance the problems of one's own selfhood against the demands of publishing and speaking out in the public sphere is what makes it an everlasting effort, constitutively unfinished and necessarily imperfect. Yet its invigorations and complexities, for me at least, make one the richer for it, even though it doesn't make one particularly popular.

II

Holding Nations and
Traditions at Bay

JULIEN BENDA'S WELL-KNOWN book *The Treason of the Intellectuals* gives the impression that intellectuals exist in a sort of universal space, bound neither by national boundaries nor by ethnic identity. It clearly seemed to Benda in 1927 that being interested in intellectuals meant being concerned only with Europeans (Jesus being the one non-European he talks about approvingly).

Things have changed a great deal since then. In the first place, Europe and the West are no longer the unchallenged standard-setters for the rest of the world. The dismantling of the great colonial empires after World War Two diminished Europe's capacity for intellectually and politically irradiating what used to be called the dark places of the earth. With the advent of the Cold War, the emergence of the Third World, and the universal emancipation implied, if not enacted, by the presence of the United Nations, non-European nations and traditions now seemed worthy of serious attention.

In the second place, the incredible speeding-up both of travel and communication has made for a new awareness of what have been called "difference" and "otherness"; in simple terms this means that if you begin to speak about intellectuals you cannot do so quite as generally as before, since for example French intellectuals are viewed as completely different in style and history from their Chinese counterparts. In other words, to speak of intellectuals today is also to speak specifically of national, religious and even continental variations on the topic, each one of which seems to require separate consideration. The African intellectuals, for instance, or the Arab intellectuals are each set in a very particular historical context, with its own problems, pathologies, triumphs, and peculiarities.

To some extent this narrowing focus and localization in the way we look at intellectuals is also due to the fantastic proliferation of specialized studies, which has quite justifiably tracked the expanding role of intellectuals in modern life. In most decent university or research libraries in the West one can turn up thousands of titles about intellectuals in various countries, each group of which would take many years to master. Then of course there are many different languages for intellectuals, some of them, like Arabic and Chinese, dictating a very special relationship between modern intellectual discourse and old, usually very rich, traditions. Here too, a Western historian trying seriously to understand intellectuals in those other, different traditions would also be required to spend years learning their languages. Yet despite all this difference and otherness, despite the inevitable erosion of the universal concept of what it means to be an intellectual, some general notions about the individual intellectual—which is my concern here—do seem to have more than strictly local application.

The first of these that I want to discuss is nationality, and with it that hothouse development from nationality, nationalism. No modern intellectual—and this is as true of major figures like Noam Chomsky and Bertrand Russell as it is of individuals whose names are not as famous—writes in Esperanto, that is, in a language designed either to belong to the whole world or to no particular country and tradition. Every individual intellectual is born into a language, and for the most part spends the rest of his or her life in that language, which is the principal medium of intellectual activity. Languages of course are always national—Greek, French, Arabic, English, German, and so forth—although one of the main points I am making here is that the intellectual is obliged to use a national language not only for obvious reasons of convenience and familiarity but also because he or she hopes to impress on the language a particular sound, a special accent, and finally a perspective that is his or her own.

The particular problem of the intellectual, however, is that a language community in each society that is dominated by habits of expression already exists, one of whose main functions is to preserve the status quo, and to make certain that things go smoothly, unchanged, and unchallenged. George Orwell talks about this very persuasively in his essay "Politics and the English Language." Clichés, tired metaphors, lazy writing, he says, are instances of "the decay of language." The result is that the mind is numbed and remains inactive while language that has the effect of background music in a supermarket washes over consciousness, seducing it into passive acceptance of unexamined ideas and sentiments.

Orwell's concern in that essay written in 1946 was the gradual encroachment on English minds of political demagogues. "Political language," he says, "—and with variations this is true of all political parties, from Conservatives to Anarchists—is designed to make lies sound truthful and murder respectable, and to give an appearance of solidity to pure wind."[1] The problem is both larger and more ordinary than that, however, and can be illustrated by looking briefly at the way language today has of tending to more general, more collective and corporate forms. Take journalism as a case in point. In the United States the bigger the scope and power of a newspaper, the more authoritative its sound, the more closely identified it is with a sense of a community larger than just a group of professional writers and readers. The difference between a tabloid and the *New York Times* is that the *Times* aspires (and is generally considered) to be the national newspaper of record, its editorials reflecting not only the opinions of a few men and women but supposedly also the perceived truth of and for the entire nation. In contrast, the tabloid is designed to capture immediate attention through sensational articles and eye-catching typography. Any article in the *New York Times* carries with it a sober authority, suggesting long

---

[1]George Orwell, *A Collection of Essays* (New York: Doubleday Anchor, 1954), p. 177.

research, careful meditation, considered judgment. The editorial use of "we" and "us" refers directly to the editors themselves of course, but simultaneously suggests a national corporate identity, as in "we the people of the United States." During the Gulf War public discussion of the crisis, especially on television but also in print journalism, assumed the existence of this national "we," which was repeated by reporters, military personnel, and ordinary citizens alike, such as "when are *we* going to begin the ground war," or 'have *we* incurred any casualties?"

Journalism only clarifies and fixes what is normally implied in the very existence of a national language like English, i.e., a national community, a national identity or self. In *Culture and Anarchy* (1869) Matthew Arnold went as far as saying that the State was the nation's best self, and a national culture the expression of the very best that had been said or thought. Far from self-evident, these best selves and best thoughts are, Arnold said, what "men of culture" are supposed to articulate and represent. He seemed to mean what I have been calling intellectuals, those individuals whose capacity for thought and judgment made them suitable for representing the best thought— culture itself—and making it prevail. Arnold is quite explicit about saying that all this is supposed to take place for the benefit not of individual classes or small groups of people but for the whole society. Here again, as is the case with modern journalism, the role of intellectuals is supposed to be that of helping a national community feel more of a sense of common identity, and a very elevated one at that.

Underlying Arnold's argument is a fear that in becoming more democratic, with more people demanding
the right to vote and the right to do what they pleased,
society was becoming more fractious, more difficult to
govern. Hence the implied need for intellectuals to calm
people down, to show them that the best ideas and the
best works of literature constituted a way of belonging to
a national community, which in turn precluded what Arnold called "doing as one likes." That was during the 1860s.

To Benda in the 1920s, intellectuals were in danger
of following Arnold's prescriptions too well. In showing
the French how great French science and literature were,
intellectuals were also teaching citizens that to belong to
a national community was an end in itself, especially if that
community was a great nation like France. Instead Benda
proposed that intellectuals should stop thinking in terms
of collective passions and should concentrate instead on
transcendental values, those that were universally appli-
cable to all nations and peoples. As I said a moment ago,
Benda took it for granted that these values were European
and not Indian or Chinese. As for the kind of intellectuals
he approved of, they too were European men.

There seems to be no way of escaping the frontiers
and enclosures built around us either by nations or by other
kinds of communities (like Europe, Africa, the West, or
Asia) that share a common language and a whole set of
implied and shared characteristics, prejudices, fixed habits
of thought. Nothing is more common in public discourse
than phrases like "the English" or "the Arabs" or "the

Americans" or "the Africans," each of them suggesting not only a whole culture but a specific mind-set.

It is very much the case today that in dealing with the Islamic world—all one billion people in it, with dozens of different societies, half a dozen major languages including Arabic, Turkish, Iranian, all of them spread out over about a third of the globe—American or British academic intellectuals speak reductively and, in my view, irresponsibly of something called "Islam." By using this single word they seem to regard Islam as a simple object about which grand generalizations spanning a millennium and a half of Muslim history can be made, and about which judgments concerning the compatibility between Islam and democracy, Islam and human rights, Islam and progress are quite unabashedly advanced.[2]

Were these discussions simply the learned animadversions of individual scholars looking, like George Eliot's Mr. Casaubon, for a Key to all Mythologies, one could dismiss them as so much occult dithering. But they take place in the post–Cold War context provided by the United States' domination of the Western alliance, in which a consensus has emerged about resurgent or fundamentalist Islam being the new threat that has replaced Communism. Here corporate thinking has *not* made intellectuals into the questioning and skeptical individual minds I have been

[2]I have discussed this practice in *Orientalism* (New York: Pantheon, 1978), *Covering Islam* (New York: Pantheon, 1981), and more recently in the *New York Times Sunday Magazine* November 21, 1993 article, "The Phoney Islamic Threat."

describing, individuals who represent not the consensus but doubts about it on rational, moral and political, to say nothing of methodological grounds, but rather into a chorus that echoes the prevailing policy view, hastening it along into more corporate thinking, and into a gradually more and more irrational sense that "we" are being threatened by "them." The result is intolerance and fear rather than knowledge and community.

But alas it is only too easy to repeat collective formulas, since merely to use a national language at all (there being no alternative to it) tends to commit you to what is readiest at hand, herding you into those stock phrases and popular metaphors for "us" and "them" that so many agencies, including journalism, academic professionalism, and expedient communal intelligibility, keep in currency. All this is part of maintaining a national identity. To feel, for example, that the Russians are coming, or that the Japanese economic invasion is upon us, or that militant Islam is on the march, is not only to experience collective alarm, but also to consolidate "our" identity as beleaguered and at risk. How to deal with this is a major question for the intellectual today. Does the fact of nationality commit the individual intellectual, who is for my purposes here the center of attention, to the public mood for reasons of solidarity, primordial loyalty, or national patriotism? Or can a better case be made for the intellectual as a dissenter from the corporate ensemble?

Never solidarity before criticism is the short answer. The intellectual always has a choice either to side with the weaker, the less well represented, the forgotten or ignored, or to side with the more powerful. Here it is good to be reminded that national languages are themselves not merely out there, sitting around for use, but must be appropriated for use. An American columnist writing during the Vietnam War, for example, using the words "us" and "our" has appropriated neutral pronouns and affiliated them consciously either with that criminal invasion of a distant Southeast Asian nation, or, a much more difficult alternative, with those lonely voices of dissent for whom the American war was both unwise and unjust. This does not mean opposition for opposition's sake. But it does mean asking questions, making distinctions, restoring to memory all those things that tend to be overlooked or walked past in the rush to collective judgment and action. With regard to the consensus on group or national identity it is the intellectual's task to show how the group is not a natural or god-given entity but is a constructed, manufactured, even in some cases invented object, with a history of struggle and conquest behind it, that it is sometimes important to represent. In the United States Noam Chomsky and Gore Vidal have performed this task with unstinting effort.

One of the finest examples of what I mean is also to be found in Virginia Woolf's essay *A Room of One's Own,* a crucial text for the modern feminist intellectual. Asked to give a lecture on women and fiction, Woolf at the outset decides that to do so beyond stating her conclusion—that a woman must have money and a room of her own if she is to write fiction—she must make of the proposition a rational argument, and this in turn commits her to a process she describes as follows: "One can only show how one came to hold whatever opinion one does hold." Exposing her argument, Woolf says, is an alternative to telling the truth directly, since where sex is concerned controversy rather than debate is likely to ensue: "one can only give one's audience the chance of drawing their own conclusions as they observe the limitations, the prejudices, the idiosyncrasies of the speaker." This is tactically disarming of course, but it also involves personal risk. That combination of vulnerability and rational argument provides Woolf with a perfect opening through which she can enter her subject, not as a dogmatic voice providing the *ipsissima verba,* but as an intellectual representing the forgotten "weaker sex," in a language perfectly suited for the job. Thus the effect of *A Room of One's Own* is to separate out from the language and power of what Woolf calls patriarchy a new sensitivity to the place, both subordinate and usually not thought about but hidden, of women. Hence the splendid pages about the Jane Austen who hid her manuscript, or the subterranean anger affecting Charlotte Brontë, or, most impressive, on the relationship between male, that is, dominant, and female, that is, secondary and occluded, values.

When Woolf describes how it is that those male values are already set when a woman takes up her pen to write, she is also describing the relationship that obtains when the individual intellectual begins to write or speak. There is always a structure of power and influence, a massed history of already articulated values and ideas, and also, and most important for the intellectual, an underside to them, ideas, values, people who, like the women writers that Woolf discusses, have not been given a room of their own. As Walter Benjamin said, "whoever has emerged victorious participates to this day in the triumphal procession in which the present rulers step over those who are lying prostrate." This rather dramatic vision of history coincides with Gramsci's, for whom social reality itself is divided between rulers and those whom they rule. I think the major choice faced by the intellectual is whether to be allied with the stability of the victors and rulers or—the more difficult path—to consider that stability as a state of emergency threatening the less fortunate with the danger of complete extinction, and take into account the experience of subordination itself, as well as the memory of forgotten voices and persons. As Benjamin says, "to articulate the past historically does not mean to recognize it 'the way it was' . . . It means to seize hold of a memory [or a presence] as it flashes up at a moment of danger."[3]

One of the canonical definitions of the modern intellectual, as provided by sociologist Edward Shils, runs as follows:

In every society . . . there are some persons with an unusual sensitivity to the sacred, an uncommon reflectiveness about the nature of their universe, and the rules which govern their society. There is in every society a minority of persons who, more than the ordinary run of their fellow-

[3]Walter Benjamin, *Illuminations,* ed. Hannah Arendt, trans. Harry Zohn (New York: Schocken Books, 1969), pp. 256, 255.

men, are enquiring, and desirous of being in frequent com-
munion with symbols which are more general than the
immediate concrete situations of everyday life, and remote
in their reference in both time and space. In this minority,
there is a need to externalize the quest in oral and written
discourse, in poetic or plastic expression, in historical rem-
iniscence or writing, in ritual performance and acts of wor-
ship. This interior need to penetrate beyond the screen of
immediate concrete experience marks the existence of the
intellectuals in every society.[4]

This is partly a restatement of Benda—that intellectuals
are a sort of clerical minority—and partly a general sociological description. Shils later adds to this that intellectuals stand at two extremes: they are either against the
prevailing norms or, in some basically accommodating way,
they exist to provide "order and continuity in public life."
My opinion is that only the first of these two possibilities
is truly the modern intellectual's role (that of disputing the
prevailing norms) precisely because the dominant norms
are today so intimately connected to (because commanded
at the top by) the nation, which is always triumphalist,
always in a position of authority, always exacting loyalty
and subservience rather than intellectual investigation and
re-examination of the kind that both Woolf and Walter
Benjamin speak about.

[4]Edward Shils, "The Intellectuals and the Powers: Some Perspectives
for Comparative Analysis," *Comparative Studies in Society and History,*
Vol. 1 (1958–59), 5–22.

Moreover, in many cultures today intellectuals principally *question,* rather than communicate directly with, the general symbols Shils speaks about. There has been a shift therefore from patriotic consensus and acquiescence, to skepticism and contest. For an American intellectual like Kirkpatrick Sale the entire narrative of perfect discovery and unlimited opportunity which had guaranteed American exceptionalism in the establishment of a new republic and was celebrated in 1992 is unacceptably flawed, because the pillage and genocide that destroyed the earlier state of affairs was too high a price to have paid.[5] Traditions and values once held as sacred now appear both hypocritical and racially based. And on many university campuses in America the debate about the canon—for all its sometimes idiotic stridency or fatuous smugness—reveals a much more unstable intellectual attitude towards national symbols, hallowed traditions, and nobly unassailable ideas. As for cultures like the Islamic or the Chinese, with their fabulous continuities and immensely secure basic symbols, there too intellectuals like Ali Shariati, Adonis, Kamal Abu Deeb, the intellectuals of the May 4th Movement, provocatively disturb the monumental calm and inviolate aloofness of the tradition.[6]

[5]This is persuasively set out in Kirkpatrick Sale, *The Conquest of Paradise: Christopher Columbus and the Columbian Legacy* (New York: Knopf, 1992).

[6]The May 4th, 1919 student movement in China occurred as an immediate response to the Versailles Conference of the same year which sanctioned Japanese presence in Shantung, when 3,000 students gathered in Tiananmen Square. This first student protest in China marked the be-

I think this is certainly as true in countries like the United States, Britain, France, Germany, where recently the very idea of national identity has been openly contested for its insufficiencies, not just by intellectuals but by an urgent demographic reality. There are now immigrant communities in Europe from the former colonial territories to whom the ideas of "France" and "Britain" and "Germany" as constituted during the period between 1800 and 1950 simply exclude them. In addition newly invigorated feminist and gay movements in all these countries also contest the patriarchal and fundamentally masculine norms regulating society hitherto. In the United States, an expanding number of recently arrived immigrants, as well as a gradually more vocal and visible population of native people—the forgotten Indians whose lands were expropriated and whose environment was either completely destroyed or totally transformed by the advancing republic—have added their testimony to those of women, African-Americans, and the sexual minorities, in order to challenge the tradition that for two centuries has been derived from the New England Puritans and the southern slave and plantation-owners. Responding to all this has been a resurgence

---

ginning of other nationwide students' organized movements in the twentieth century. Thirty-two students were arrested and this led to a fresh mobilization of students for their release as much as for firm government action over the Shantung issue. The government's attempt to suppress the students' movement failed as the movement gained support from China's emerging entrepreneurial class that was threatened by Japanese competition. See John Israel, *Student Nationalism in China, 1927–1937* (Stanford: Stanford University Press, 1966).

of appeals to a tradition, to patriotism and to basic, or family, values as Vice-President Dan Quayle called them, all of them associated with a past that is no longer recoverable except by denying or somehow downgrading the lived experience of those who, in Aimé Césaire's great phrase, want a place at the rendezvous of victory.[7]

Even in a large number of countries of the Third World a clamorous antagonism between the status quo powers of the national state and the disadvantaged populations locked inside, but unrepresented or suppressed by it, provides the intellectual with a real opportunity to resist the forward march of the victors. In the Arab-Islamic world a still more complicated situation obtains. Countries like Egypt and Tunisia, which have long been ruled since independence by secular nationalist parties that have now degenerated into coteries and cliques, are suddenly rent by Islamic groups whose mandate, they say with considerable justice, is granted them by the oppressed, the urban poor, the landless peasants of the countryside, all those with no hope except a restored or reconstructed Islamic past. Many people are willing to fight to the death for these ideas.

But Islam is the majority religion after all, and simply to say that "Islam is the way," leveling most dissent and difference, to say nothing of widely divergent interpretations of Islam, is not, I believe, the intellectual's role. Islam after all is a religion and culture, both of them composite

---

[7] Aimé Césaire, *The Collected Poetry,* trans. Clayton Eshelman and Annette Smith (Berkeley: University of California Press, 1983), p. 72.

and very far from monolithic. Yet insofar as it is the faith
and identity of the vast majority of people it is by no means
incumbent on the intellectual simply to go in for choruses
praising Islam, but rather to introduce into the din, first
of all, an interpretation of Islam stressing its complex, het-
erodox nature—Islam of the rulers, asks Adonis, the Syrian
poet and intellectual, or of the dissenting poets and
sects?—and second, asking Islamic authorities to face the
challenges of non-Islamic minorities, women's rights, of
modernity itself, with humane attentiveness and honest
reappraisals, not dogmatic or pseudo-populist chants. The
nub of this for the intellectual in Islam is a revival of *ijtihad,*
personal interpretation, and not a sheeplike abdication to
politically ambitious *'ulema* or charismatic demagogues.

Always, however, the intellectual is beset and remorselessly challenged by the problem of loyalty. All of
us without exception belong to some sort of national, religious or ethnic community: no one, no matter the volume
of protestations, is above the organic ties that bind the
individual to family, community, and of course nationality.
For an emergent and beset group—say, the Bosnians or
the Palestinians today—feeling that your people are threatened with political and sometimes actual physical extinction commits you to its defense, to doing everything within
your power to protect, or to fight against the national enemies. This is defensive nationalism, of course; yet as Frantz
Fanon analyzed the situation during the height of the Algerian war of liberation (1954–1962) against the French,
going along with the approving chorus of anticolonialist
nationalism as embodied in party and leadership is not

enough. There is always the question of goal which, even in the thick of battle, entails the analysis of choices. Are we fighting just to rid ourselves of colonialism, a necessary goal, or are we thinking about what we will do when the last white policeman leaves?

According to Fanon, the goal of the native intellectual cannot simply be to replace a white policeman with his native counterpart, but rather what he called, borrowing from Aimé Césaire, the invention of new souls. In other words, although there is inestimable value to what an intellectual does to ensure the community's survival during periods of extreme national emergency, loyalty to the group's fight for survival cannot draw in the intellectual so far as to narcotize the critical sense, or reduce its imperatives, which are always to go beyond survival to questions of political liberation, to critiques of the leadership, to presenting alternatives that are too often marginalized or pushed aside as irrelevant to the main battle at hand. Even among the oppressed there are also victors and losers, and the intellectual's loyalty must not be restricted only to joining the collective march: great intellectuals like Tagore of India or Jose Martí of Cuba were exemplary in this regard, never abating their criticism *because* of nationalism, even though they remained nationalists themselves.

In no country more than modern Japan has the interplay between the imperatives of the collective and the problem of intellectual alignment been so tragically problematic and vexed. The Meiji Restoration of 1868 that brought back the emperor was followed by the abolition of feudalism, and the deliberate course of building a new composite ideology began. This led disastrously to fascist militarism and national perdition that culminated in the defeat of imperial Japan in 1945. As the historian Carol Gluck has argued, the *tennosei ideorogii* (emperor ideology) was the creation of intellectuals during the Meiji period, and while it was originally nurtured by a sense of national defensiveness, even inferiority, in 1915 it had become a full-fledged nationalism capable simultaneously of extreme militarism, veneration of the emperor, and a sort of nativism that subordinated the individual to the state.[8] It also denigrated other races to such an extent as to permit the willful slaughter of Chinese in the 1930s, for example, in the name of *shido minzeku,* the idea that the Japanese were the leading race.

One of the most shameful episodes in the modern history of intellectuals took place during World War Two when, as John Dower has described it, Japanese and American intellectuals joined the battle of national and racial name-calling on an offensive and ultimately debasing scale.[9] After the war, most Japanese intellectuals according to Masao Miyoshi were convinced that the essence of their new mission was not just the dismantling of *tennosei* (or corporate) ideology, but the construction of a liberal individualist subjectivity—*shutaisei*—meant to compete with the West, but alas doomed, Miyoshi says, to "the ultimate consumerist vacuity in which the act of buying

[8]See Carol Gluck, *Japan's Modern Myths: Ideology in the Late Meiji Period* (Princeton: Princeton University Press, 1985).
[9]John Dower, *War Without Mercy: Race and Power in the Pacific War* (New York: Pantheon, 1986).

alone serves as the confirmation and reassurance of individual beings." Miyoshi reminds us, however, that postwar intellectual attention given to the matter of subjectivity also included giving voice to questions of responsibility for the war, as in the works of the writer Maruyama Masao, who spoke effectively of an intellectual "community of penitence."[10]

In dark times an intellectual is very often looked to by members of his or her nationality to represent, speak out for, and testify to the sufferings of that nationality. Prominent intellectuals always are, to use Oscar Wilde's description of himself, in symbolic relationship with their time: in the public consciousness they represent achievement, fame, and reputation which can be mobilized on behalf of an ongoing struggle or embattled community. Inversely, prominent intellectuals are very often made to bear the brunt of their community's opprobrium, either when factions within it associate the intellectual with the wrong side (this has been quite common in Ireland, for instance, but also in Western metropolitan centers during the Cold War years when pro- and anti-Communists traded blows) or when other groups mobilize for an attack. Certainly Wilde felt himself to be suffering the guilt of all avant-garde thinkers who had dared to challenge the norms

[10]Masao Miyoshi, *Off Center: Power and Culture Relations Between Japan and the United States* (Cambridge, Mass.: Harvard University Press, 1991), pp. 125, 108. Maruyama Masao is a postwar Japanese writer and a leading critic of Japanese imperial history and the emperor system; Miyoshi describes him as too accepting of the West's aesthetic and intellectual predominance.

of middle-class society. In our own time a man like Elie Wiesel has come to symbolize the sufferings of the six million Jews who were exterminated in the Nazi Holocaust.

To this terribly important task of representing the collective suffering of your own people, testifying to its travails, reasserting its enduring presence, reinforcing its memory, there must be added something else, which only an intellectual, I believe, has the obligation to fulfill. After all, many novelists, painters, and poets, like Manzoni, Picasso, or Neruda, have embodied the historical experience of their people in aesthetic works, which in turn become recognized as great masterpieces. For the intellectual the task, I believe, is explicitly to universalize the crisis, to give greater human scope to what a particular race or nation suffered, to associate that experience with the sufferings of others.

It is inadequate only to affirm that a people was dispossessed, oppressed or slaughtered, denied its rights and its political existence, without at the same time doing what Fanon did during the Algerian war, affiliating those horrors with the similar afflictions of other people. This does not at all mean a loss in historical specificity, but rather it guards against the possibility that a lesson learned about oppression in one place will be forgotten or violated in another place or time. And just because you represent the sufferings that your people lived through which you yourself might have lived through also, you are not relieved of the duty of revealing that your own people now may be visiting related crimes on *their* victims.

The South African Boers, for instance, have seen themselves as the victims of British imperialism; but this meant that after surviving British "aggression" during the Boer War, the Boers as a community represented by Daniel François Malan felt themselves entitled to assert their historical experience by setting up through the doctrines of the National Party what became apartheid. It is always easy and popular for intellectuals to fall into modes of vindication and self-righteousness that blind them to the evil done in the name of their own ethnic or national community. This is particularly true during periods of emergency and crisis, when rallying to the flag during the Falklands or Vietnamese wars, for example, meant that debate on the justice of a war was construed as the equivalent of treason. But though nothing can make you more unpopular, an intellectual must speak out against that sort of gregariousness, and the personal cost be damned.

III

Intellectual Exile:
Expatriates and Marginals

EXILE IS ONE of the saddest fates. In premodern times banishment was a particularly dreadful punishment since it not only meant years of aimless wandering away from family and familiar places, but also meant being a sort of permanent outcast, someone who never felt at home, and was always at odds with the environment, inconsolable about the past, bitter about the present and the future. There has always been an association between the idea of exile and the terrors of being a leper, a social and moral untouchable. During the twentieth century, exile has been transformed from the exquisite, and sometimes exclusive, punishment of special individuals—like the great Latin poet Ovid, who was banished from Rome to a remote town on the Black Sea—into a cruel punishment of whole communities and peoples, often the inadvertent result of impersonal forces such as war, famine, and disease.

In this category are the Armenians, a gifted but frequently displaced people who lived in large numbers throughout the eastern Mediterranean (Anatolia especially) but who after genocidal attacks on them by the Turks flooded nearby Beirut, Aleppo, Jerusalem and Cairo, only to be dislocated again during the revolutionary upheavals of the post–World War Two period. I have long been deeply drawn to those large expatriate or exile communities who peopled the landscape of my youth in Palestine and Egypt. There were many Armenians of course, but also Jews, Italians, and Greeks who, once settled in the Levant, had grown productive roots there—these communities after all produced prominent writers like Edmond Jabes, Giuseppe Ungaretti, Constantine Cavafy—that were to be brutally torn up after the establishment of Israel in 1948 and after the Suez war of 1956. To new nationalist governments in Egypt and Iraq and elsewhere in the Arab world, foreigners who symbolized the new aggression of European postwar imperialism were forced to leave, and for many old communities this was a particularly nasty fate. Some of these were acclimatized to new places of residence, but many were, in a manner of speaking, re-exiled.

There is a popular but wholly mistaken assumption that being exiled is to be totally cut off, isolated, hopelessly separated from your place of origin. Would that surgically clean separation were true, because then at least you could have the consolation of knowing that what you have left behind is, in a sense, unthinkable and completely irrecoverable. The fact is that for most exiles the difficulty consists not simply in being forced to live away from home, but rather, given today's world, in living with the many reminders that you are in exile, that your home is not in fact so far away, and that the normal traffic of everyday contemporary life keeps you in constant but tantalizing and unfulfilled touch with the old place. The exile therefore exists in a median state, neither completely at one with the new setting nor fully disencumbered of the old, beset with half-involvements and half-detachments, nostalgic and sentimental on one level, an adept mimic or a secret outcast on another. Being skilled at survival becomes the main imperative, with the danger of getting too comfortable and secure constituting a threat that is constantly to be guarded against.

Salim, the main character of V. S. Naipaul's novel *A Bend in the River*, is an affecting instance of the modern intellectual in exile: an East African Muslim of Indian origin, he has left the coast and journeyed towards the African interior, where he has survived precariously in a new state modeled on Mobuto's Zaire. Naipaul's extraordinary antennae as a novelist enable him to portray Salim's life at a "bend in the river" as a sort of no-man's-land, to which come the European intellectual advisers (who succeed the idealistic missionaries of colonial times), as well as the mercenaries, profiteers, and other Third World flotsam and jetsam in whose ambiance Salim is forced to live, gradually losing his property and his integrity in the mounting confusion. By the end of the novel—and this of course is Naipaul's debatable ideological point—even the natives have become exiles in their own country, so preposterous and erratic are the whims of the ruler, Big Man, who is intended by Naipaul to be a symbol of all postcolonial regimes.

The widespread territorial rearrangements of the post–World War Two period produced huge demographic movements, for example, the Indian Muslims who moved to Pakistan after the 1947 partition, or the Palestinians who were largely dispersed during Israel's establishment to accommodate incoming European and Asian Jews; and these transformations in turn gave rise to hybrid political forms. In Israel's political life there has been not only a politics of the Jewish diaspora but also an intertwining and competing politics of the Palestinian people in exile. In the newly founded countries of Pakistan and Israel the recent immigrants were seen as part of an exchange of populations, but politically they were also regarded as formerly oppressed minorities enabled to live in their new states as members of the majority. Yet far from settling sectarian issues, partition and the separatist ideology of new statehood have rekindled and often inflamed them. My concern here is more with the largely unaccommodated exiles, like Palestinians or the new Muslim immigrants in continental Europe, or the West Indian and African blacks in England, whose presence complicates the presumed homogeneity of the new societies in which they live. The intellectual who considers him- or herself to be a part of a more general condition affecting the displaced national community is therefore likely to be a source not of acculturation and adjustment, but rather of volatility and instability.

This is by no means to say that exile doesn't also produce marvels of adjustment. The United States today is in the unusual position of having two extremely high

former officers in recent presidential administrations—
Henry Kissinger and Zbigniew Brzezinski—who were (or
still are, depending on the observer's outlook) intellectuals
in exile, Kissinger from Nazi Germany, Brzezinski from
Communist Poland. In addition Kissinger is Jewish, which
puts him in the extraordinarily odd position of also qualifying for potential immigration to Israel, according to its
Basic Law of Return. Yet both Kissinger and Brzezinski
seem on the surface at least to have contributed their talents entirely to their adopted country, with results in em-
inence, material rewards, national, not to say worldwide,
influence that are light-years away from the marginal ob-
scurity in which Third World exile intellectuals live in Europe or the U.S. Today, having served in government for
several decades, the two prominent intellectuals are now
consultants to corporations and other governments.

Brzezinski and Kissinger are not perhaps as socially
exceptional as one would assume if it is recalled that the
European theater of World War Two was considered by
other exiles—like Thomas Mann—as a battle for Western
destiny, the Western soul. In this "good war" the U.S.
played the role of savior, also providing refuge for a whole
generation of scholars, artists and scientists who had fled
Western fascism for the metropolis of the new Western
imperium. In scholarly fields like the humanities and social
sciences a large group of extremely distinguished scholars
came to America. Some of them, like the great Romance
philologists and scholars of comparative literature Leo
Spitzer and Erich Auerbach, enriched American universities with their talents and Old World experience. Others,

among them scientists like Edward Teller and Werner von Braun, entered the Cold War lists as new Americans dedicated to winning the arms and space race over the Soviet Union. So all-engrossing was this concern after the war that, as has recently been revealed, well-placed American intellectuals in the social sciences managed to recruit former Nazis known for their anti-Communist credentials to work in the U.S. as part of the great crusade.

Along with the rather shady art of political trimming, a technique of not taking a clear position but surviving handsomely nonetheless, how an intellectual works out an accommodation with a new or emerging dominant power is a topic I shall deal with in my next two lectures. Here I want to focus on its opposite, the intellectual who because of exile cannot, or, more to the point, will not make the adjustment, preferring instead to remain outside the mainstream, unaccommodated, unco-opted, resistant: but first I need to make some preliminary points.

One is that while it is an *actual* condition, exile is also for my purposes a *metaphorical* condition. By that I mean that my diagnosis of the intellectual in exile derives from the social and political history of dislocation and migration with which I began this lecture, but is not limited to it. Even intellectuals who are lifelong members of a society can, in a manner of speaking, be divided into insiders and outsiders: those on the one hand who belong fully to the society as it is, who flourish in it without an overwhelming sense of dissonance or dissent, those who can be called yea-sayers; and on the other hand, the nay-sayers, the individuals at odds with their society and therefore outsiders

and exiles so far as privileges, power, and honors are concerned. The pattern that sets the course for the intellectual
as outsider is best exemplified by the condition of exile,
the state of never being fully adjusted, always feeling outside the chatty, familiar world inhabited by natives, so to
speak, tending to avoid and even dislike the trappings of
accommodation and national well-being. Exile for the intellectual in this metaphysical sense is restlessness, movement, constantly being unsettled, and unsettling others.
You cannot go back to some earlier and perhaps more
stable condition of being at home; and, alas, you can never
fully arrive, be at one with your new home or situation.

Secondly—and I find myself somewhat surprised by
this observation even as I make it—the intellectual as exile
tends to be happy with the idea of unhappiness, so that
dissatisfaction bordering on dyspepsia, a kind of curmud-
geonly disagreeableness, can become not only a style of
thought, but also a new, if temporary, habitation. The intellectual as ranting Thersites perhaps. A great historical
prototype for what I have in mind is a powerful eighteenth-
century figure, Jonathan Swift, who never got over his fall
from influence and prestige in England after the Tories
left office in 1714, and spent the rest of his life as an exile
in Ireland. An almost legendary figure of bitterness and
anger—*saeve indignatio* he said of himself in his own ep-
itaph—Swift was furious at Ireland, and yet its defender
against British tyranny, a man whose towering Irish works
Gulliver's Travels and *The Drapier's Letters* show a mind
flourishing, not to say benefiting, from such productive
anguish.

To some degree the early V. S. Naipaul, the essayist
and travel writer, resident off and on in England, yet always on the move, revisiting his Caribbean and Indian
roots, sifting through the debris of colonialism and post-
colonialism, remorselessly judging the illusions and cruel-
ties of independent states and the new true believers, was
a figure of modern intellectual exile.

Even more rigorous, more determinedly the exile
than Naipaul, is Theodor Wiesengrund Adorno. He was
a forbidding but endlessly fascinating man, and for me,
the dominating intellectual conscience of the middle twentieth century, whose entire career skirted and fought the
dangers of fascism, communism and Western mass-
consumerism. Unlike Naipaul, who has wandered in and out
of former homes in the Third World, Adorno was completely European, a man entirely made up of the highest
of high cultures that included astonishing professional competence in philosophy, music (he was a student and admirer
of Berg and Schoenberg), sociology, literature, history, and
cultural analysis. Of partially Jewish background, he left his
native Germany in the mid-1930s shortly after the Nazi seiz-
ure of power: he went first to read philosophy at Oxford,
which is where he wrote an extremely difficult book on
Husserl. He seems to have been miserable there, surrounded
as he was by ordinary language and positivist philosophers,
he with his Spenglerian gloom and metaphysical dialectics
in the best Hegelian manner. He returned to Germany for
a while but, as a member of the University of Frankfurt
Institute of Social Research, reluctantly decamped for the
safety of the United States, where he lived for a time first

in New York (1938–41) and then in southern California.

Although Adorno returned to Frankfurt in 1949 to take up his old professorship there, his years in America stamped him with the marks of exile forever. He detested jazz and everything about popular culture; he had no affection for the landscape at all; he seems to have remained studiously mandarin in his ways; and therefore, because he was brought up in a Marxist-Hegelian philosophical tradition, everything about the worldwide influence of American films, industry, habits of daily life, fact-based learning, and pragmatism raised his hackles. Naturally Adorno was very predisposed to being a metaphysical exile before he came to the United States: he was already extremely critical of what passed for bourgeois taste in Europe, and his standards of what, for instance, music ought to have been were set by the extraordinarily difficult works of Schoenberg, works which Adorno averred were honorably destined to remain unheard and impossible to listen to. Paradoxical, ironic, mercilessly critical: Adorno was the quintessential intellectual, hating *all* systems, whether on our side or theirs, with equal distaste. For him life was at its most false in the aggregate—the whole is always the untrue, he once said—and this, he continued, placed an even greater premium on subjectivity, on the individual's consciousness, on what could not be regimented in the totally administered society.

But it was his American exile that produced Adorno's great masterpiece, the *Minima Moralia,* a set of 153 fragments published in 1953, and subtitled "Reflections from Damaged Life." In the episodic and mystifyingly eccentric form of this book, which is neither sequential autobiography nor thematic musing nor even a systematic exposé of its author's worldview, we are reminded once again of the peculiarities of Bazarov's life as represented in Turgenev's novel of Russian life in the mid-1860s, *Fathers and Sons*. The prototype of the modern nihilistic intellectual, Bazarov is given no narrative context by Turgenev; he appears briefly, then he disappears. We see him briefly with his aged parents, but it is very clear that he has deliberately cut himself off from them. We deduce from this that by virtue of living a life according to different norms, the intellectual does not have a story, but only a sort of destabilizing effect; he sets off seismic shocks, he jolts people, but he can neither be explained away by his background nor his friends.

Turgenev himself actually says nothing of this at all: he lets it happen before our eyes, as if to say that the intellectual is not only a being set apart from parents and children, but that his modes of life, his procedures of engaging with it are necessarily allusive, and can only be represented realistically as a series of discontinuous performances. Adorno's *Minima Moralia* seems to follow the same logic, although after Auschwitz, Hiroshima, the onset of the Cold War, and the triumph of America, representing the intellectual honestly is a much more tortuous thing than doing what Turgenev had done for Bazarov a hundred years earlier.

The core of Adorno's representation of the intellectual as a permanent exile, dodging both the old and the new with equal dexterity, is a writing style that is mannered and worked over in the extreme. It is fragmentary first of all, jerky, discontinuous; there is no plot or predetermined order to follow. It represents the intellectual's consciousness as unable to be at rest anywhere, constantly on guard against the blandishments of success, which, for the perversely inclined Adorno, means trying consciously *not* to be understood easily and immediately. Nor is it possible to retreat into complete privacy, since as Adorno says much later in his career, the hope of the intellectual is not that he will have an effect on the world, but that someday, somewhere, someone will read what he wrote exactly as he wrote it.

One fragment, number 18 in *Minima Moralia,* captures the significance of exile quite perfectly. "Dwelling, in the proper sense," says Adorno, "is now impossible. The traditional residences we have grown up in have grown intolerable: each trait of comfort in them is paid for with a betrayal of knowledge, each vestige of shelter with the musty pact of family interests." So much for the prewar life of people who grew up before Nazism. Socialism and American consumerism are no better: there "people live if not in slums, in bungalows that by tomorrow may be leaf-huts, trailers, cars, camps, or the open air." Thus, Adorno states, "the house is past [i.e. over]. . . . The best mode of conduct, in face of all this, still seems an uncommitted, suspended one. . . . *It is part of morality not to be at home in one's home.*"

Yet no sooner has he reached an apparent conclusion than Adorno reverses it: "But the thesis of this paradox leads to destruction, a loveless disregard for things which necessarily turns against people too; and the antithesis, no sooner uttered, is an ideology for those wishing with a bad conscience to keep what they have. Wrong life cannot be lived rightly."[1]

In other words, there is no real escape, even for the exile who tries to remain suspended, since that state of in-betweenness can itself become a rigid ideological position, a sort of dwelling whose falseness is covered over in time, and to which one can all too easily become accustomed. Yet Adorno presses on. "Suspicious probing is always salutary," especially where the intellectual's writing is concerned. "For a man who no longer has a homeland, writing becomes a place to live," yet even so—and this is Adorno's final touch—there can be no slackening of rigor in self-analysis:

> The demand that one harden oneself against self-pity implies the technical necessity to counter any slackening of intellectual tension with the utmost alertness, and to eliminate anything that has begun to encrust the work [or writing] or to drift along idly, which may at an earlier stage have served, as gossip, to generate the warm atmosphere conducive to growth, but is now left behind, flat and stale. In the end, the writer is not allowed to live in his writing.[2]

This is typically gloomy and unyielding. Adorno the intellectual in exile heaping sarcasm on the idea that one's

---

[1]Theodor Adorno, *Minima Moralia: Reflections from Damaged Life,* trans. E. F. N. Jephcott (London: New Left Books, 1951), pp. 38–39.
[2]Ibid., p. 87.

own work can provide some satisfaction, an alternative type of living that might be a slight respite from the anxiety and marginality of no "dwelling" at all. What Adorno doesn't speak about are indeed the pleasures of exile, those different arrangements of living and eccentric angles of vision that it can sometimes afford, which enliven the intellectual's vocation, without perhaps alleviating every last anxiety or feeling of bitter solitude. So while it is true to say that exile is the condition that characterizes the intellectual as someone who stands as a marginal figure outside the comforts of privilege, power, being-at-homeness (so to speak), it is also very important to stress that that condition carries with it certain rewards and, yes, even privileges. So while you are neither winning prizes nor being welcomed into all those self-congratulating honor societies that routinely exclude embarrassing troublemakers who do not toe the party line, you *are* at the same time deriving some positive things from exile and marginality.

One of course is the pleasure of being surprised, of never taking anything for granted, of learning to make do in circumstances of shaky instability that would confound or terrify most people. An intellectual is fundamentally about knowledge and freedom. Yet these acquire meaning not as abstractions—as in the rather banal statement "You must get a good education so that you can enjoy a good life"—but as experiences actually lived through. An intellectual is like a shipwrecked person who learns how to live in a certain sense *with* the land, not *on* it, not like Robinson Crusoe whose goal is to colonize his little island, but more like Marco Polo, whose sense of the marvelous never fails him, and who is always a traveler, a provisional guest, not a freeloader, conqueror, or raider.

Because the exile sees things both in terms of what has been left behind and what is actual here and now, there is a double perspective that never sees things in isolation. Every scene or situation in the new country necessarily draws on its counterpart in the old country. Intellectually this means that an idea or experience is always counterposed with another, therefore making them both appear in a sometimes new and unpredictable light: from that juxtaposition one gets a better, perhaps even more universal idea of how to think, say, about a human rights issue in one situation by comparison with another. I have felt that most of the alarmist and deeply flawed discussions of Islamic fundamentalism in the West have been intellectually invidious precisely because they have not been compared with Jewish or Christian fundamentalism, both equally prevalent and reprehensible in my own experience of the Middle East. What is usually thought of as a simple issue of judgment against an approved enemy, in double or exile perspective impels a Western intellectual to see a much wider picture, with the requirement now of taking a position as a secularist (or not) on *all* theocratic tendencies, not just against the conventionally designated ones.

A second advantage to what in effect is the exile standpoint for an intellectual is that you tend to see things not simply as they are, but as they have come to be that way. Look at situations as contingent, not as inevitable, look at them as the result of a series of historical choices made by men and women, as facts of society made by human beings, and not as natural or god-given, therefore unchangeable, permanent, irreversible.

The great prototype for this sort of intellectual position is provided by the eighteenth-century Italian philosopher Giambattista Vico, who has long been a hero of mine. Vico's great discovery, which derived in part from his loneliness as an obscure Neapolitan professor, scarcely able to survive, at odds with the Church and his immediate surroundings, is that the proper way to understand social reality is to understand it as a process generated from its point of origin, which one can always locate in extremely humble circumstances. This, he said in his great work *The New Science,* meant seeing things as having evolved from definite beginnings, as the adult human being derives from the babbling child.

Vico argues that this is the only point of view to take about the secular world, which he repeats over and over again is historical, with its own laws and processes, not divinely ordained. This entails respect, but not reverence, for human society. You look at the grandest of powers in terms of its beginnings, and where it might be headed; you are not awed by the august personality, or the magnificent institution which to a native, someone who has always seen (and therefore venerated) the grandeur but not the perforce humbler *human* origins from which it derived, often compels silence and stunned subservience. The intellectual in exile is necessarily ironic, skeptical, even playful—but not cynical.

Finally, as any real exile will confirm, once you leave your home, wherever you end up you cannot simply take up life and become just another citizen of the new place. Or if you do, there is a good deal of awkwardness involved in the effort, which scarcely seems worth it. You can spend a lot of time regretting what you lost, envying those around you who have always been at home, near their loved ones, living in the place where they were born and grew up without ever having to experience not only the loss of what was once theirs, but above all the torturing memory of a life to which they cannot return. On the other hand, as Rilke once said, you can become a beginner in your circumstances, and this allows you an unconventional style of life, and above all, a different, often very eccentric career.

For the intellectual an exilic displacement means being liberated from the usual career, in which "doing well" and following in time-honored footsteps are the main milestones. Exile means that you are always going to be marginal, and that what you do as an intellectual has to be made up because you cannot follow a prescribed path. If you can experience that fate not as a deprivation and as something to be bewailed, but as a sort of freedom, a process of discovery in which you do things according to your own pattern, as various interests seize your attention, and as the particular goal you set yourself dictates: that is a unique pleasure. You see it in the odyssey of C. L. R. James, the Trinidadian essayist and historian, who came to England as a cricket player between the two World Wars and whose intellectual autobiography, *Beyond a Boundary,* was an account of his life in cricket, and of cricket in colonialism. His other work included *The Black Jacobins,* a stirring history of the late-eighteenth-century Haitian black slave revolt led by Toussaint L'Ouverture; being an orator and political organizer in America; writing a study of Herman Melville, *Mariners, Renegades, and Castaways,* plus various works on pan-Africanism, and dozens of essays on popular culture and literature. An eccentric, unsettled course, so unlike anything we would today call a solid professional career, and yet what exuberance and unending self-discovery it contains.

Most of us may not be able to duplicate the destiny of exiles like Adorno or C. L. R. James, but their significance for the contemporary intellectual is nevertheless very pertinent. Exile is a model for the intellectual who is tempted, and even beset and overwhelmed, by the rewards of accommodation, yea-saying, settling in. Even if one is not an actual immigrant or expatriate, it is still possible to think as one, to imagine and investigate in spite of barriers, and always to move away from the centralizing authorities towards the margins, where you see things that are usually lost on minds that have never traveled beyond the conventional and the comfortable.

A condition of marginality, which might seem irresponsible or flippant, frees you from having always to proceed with caution, afraid to overturn the applecart, anxious about upsetting fellow members of the same corporation. No one is ever free of attachments and sentiments of course. Nor do I have in mind here the so-called free-floating intellectual, whose technical competence is on loan and for sale to anyone. I am saying, however, that to be as marginal and as undomesticated as someone who is in real exile is for an intellectual to be unusually responsive to the traveler rather than to the potentate, to the provisional and risky rather than to the habitual, to innovation and experiment rather than the authoritatively given *status quo.* The *exilic* intellectual does not respond to the logic of the conventional but to the audacity of daring, and to representing change, to moving on, not standing still.

IV

Professionals and Amateurs

IN 1979 THE versatile and ingenious French intellectual Regis Debray published a penetrating account of French cultural life entitled *Teachers, Writers, Celebrities: The Intellectuals of Modern France.*[1] Debray himself had once been a seriously committed left-wing activist who had taught at the University of Havana shortly after the Cuban Revolution of 1958. Some years later, the Bolivian authorities gave him a thirty-year prison term because of his association with Che Guevara, but he served only three years. After his return to France, Debray became a semi-academic political analyst and later still an adviser to President Mitterand. He was thus uniquely placed to understand the relationship between intellectuals and institutions, which is never static but always evolving and sometimes surprising in its complexity.

[1]Regis Debray, *Teachers, Writers, Celebrities: The Intellectuals of Modern France*, trans. David Macey (London: New Left Books, 1981).

Debray's thesis in the book is that between 1880 and 1930 Parisian intellectuals were principally connected to the Sorbonne; they were secular refugees from both church and Bonapartism, where in laboratories, libraries, and classrooms the intellectual was protected as a professor and could make important advances in knowledge. After 1930 the Sorbonne slowly lost its authority to new publishing houses like the Nouvelle Revue Française, where according to Debray "the spiritual family" comprising the intelligentsia and their editors was given a more hospitable roof over its head. Until roughly 1960, such writers as Sartre, de Beauvoir, Camus, Mauriac, Gide, and Malraux were in effect the intelligentsia who had superseded the professoriate because of their free-ranging work, their credo of freedom, and their discourse that was "mid-way between the ecclesiastical solemnity that went before it and the shrillness of the advertising that came after."[2]

Around 1968 intellectuals largely deserted their publishers' fold; instead they flocked to the mass media—as journalists, talk-show guests and hosts, advisers, managers, and so on. Not only did they now have a huge mass audience, but also their entire lifework as intellectuals depended on their viewers, on acclaim or oblivion as given by those "others" who had become a faceless consuming audience out there. "By extending the reception area, the mass media have reduced the sources of intellectual legitimacy, surrounding the professional intelligentsia, the classic source of legitimacy, with wider concentric circles that

[2]Ibid., p. 71.

are less demanding and therefore more easily won over. . . . The mass media have broken down the closure of the traditional intelligentsia, together with its evaluative norms and its scale of values."[3]

What Debray describes is almost entirely a local French situation, the result of a struggle between secular, imperial and ecclesiastical forces in that society since Napoleon. It is therefore most unlikely that the picture he gives of France would be found in other countries. In Britain, for example, the major universities before World War Two could hardly be characterized in Debray's terms. Even Oxford and Cambridge dons were not principally known in the public domain as intellectuals in the French sense; and although British publishing houses were powerful and influential between the two World Wars, they and their authors did not constitute the spiritual family Debray speaks about in France. Nevertheless the general point is a valid one: groups of individuals are aligned with institutions and derive power and authority from those institutions. As the institutions either rise or fall in ascendancy, so too do their organic intellectuals, to use Antonio's Gramsci's serviceable phrase for them.

And yet the question remains as to whether there is or can be anything like an independent, autonomously functioning intellectual, one who is not beholden to, and therefore constrained by, his or her affiliations with universities that pay salaries, political parties that demand loyalty to a party line, think tanks that while they offer

[3]Ibid., p. 81.

freedom to do research perhaps more subtly compromise judgment and restrain the critical voice. As Debray suggests, once an intellectual's circle is widened beyond a like group of intellectuals—in other words, when worry about pleasing an audience or an employer replaces dependence on other intellectuals for debate and judgment—something in the intellectual's vocation is, if not abrogated, then certainly inhibited.

We come back once again to my main theme, the representation of the intellectual. When we think of an individual intellectual—and the individual is my principal concern here—do we accentuate the individuality of the person in drawing his or her portrait, or do we rather make our focus the group or class of which the individual is a member? The answer to this question obviously affects our expectations of the intellectual's address to us: is what we hear or read an independent view, or does it represent a government, an organized political cause, a lobbying group? Nineteenth-century representations of the intellectual tended to stress individuality, the fact that very often the intellectual is, like Turgenev's Bazarov or James Joyce's Stephen Dedalus, a solitary, somehow aloof figure, who does not conform to society at all and is consequently a rebel completely outside established opinion. With the increased number of twentieth-century men and women who belong to a general group called intellectuals or the intelligentsia—the managers, professors, journalists, computer or government experts, lobbyists, pundits, syndicated columnists, consultants who are paid for their opinions—one is impelled to wonder whether the individual intellectual as an independent voice can exist at all.

This is a tremendously important question and must be looked into with a combination of realism and idealism, certainly not cynicism. A cynic, Oscar Wilde says, is someone who knows the price of everything but the value of nothing. To accuse all intellectuals of being sellouts just because they earn their living working in a university or for a newspaper is a coarse and finally meaningless charge. It would be far too indiscriminately cynical to say that the world is so corrupt that everyone ultimately succumbs to Mammon. On the other hand, it is scarcely less serious to hold up the individual intellectual as a perfect ideal, a sort of shining knight who is so pure and so noble as to deflect any suspicion of material interest. No one can pass such a test, not even Joyce's Stephen Dedalus, who is so pure and fiercely ideal that he is in the end to be incapacitated and, even worse, silent.

The fact is that the intellectual ought neither to be so uncontroversial and safe a figure as to be just a friendly technician nor should the intellectual try to be a full-time Cassandra, who was not only righteously unpleasant but also unheard. Every human being is held in by a society, no matter how free and open the society, no matter how bohemian the individual. In any case, the intellectual is supposed to be heard from, and in practice ought to be stirring up debate and if possible controversy. But the alternatives are not total quiescence or total rebelliousness.

During the waning days of the Reagan administration a disaffected left-wing American intellectual called Russell Jacoby published a book that generated a great deal of discussion, much of it approving. It was called *The Last Intellectuals,* and argued the unimpeachable thesis that in the United States "the non-academic intellectual" had completely disappeared, leaving no one in that place except a whole bunch of timid and jargon-ridden university dons, to whom no one in the society paid very much attention.[4] Jacoby's model for the intellectual of yore was comprised of a few names that lived mostly in Greenwich Village (the local equivalent of the Latin Quarter) earlier this century and were known by the general name of the New York intellectuals. Most of them were Jewish, left-wing (but mostly anti-Communist), and managed to live by their pens. Figures of the earlier generation included men and women like Edmund Wilson, Jane Jacobs, Lewis Mumford, Dwight McDonald; their slightly later counterparts were Philip Rahv, Alfred Kazin, Irving Howe, Susan Sontag, Daniel Bell, William Barrett, Lionel Trilling. According to Jacoby the likes of such people have been diminished by various postwar social and political forces: the flight to the suburbs (Jacoby's point being that the intellectual is an urban creature), the irresponsibilities of the Beat generation, who pioneered the idea of dropping out and fleeing from their appointed station in life; the expansion of the university; and the drift to the campus of the former American independent Left.

The result is that today's intellectual is most likely to be a closeted literature professor, with a secure income,

---

[4]Russell Jacoby, *The Last Intellectuals: American Culture in the Age of Academe* (New York: Basic Books, 1987).

and no interest in dealing with the world outside the class-room. Such individuals, Jacoby alleges, write an esoteric and barbaric prose that is meant mainly for academic advancement and not for social change. Meanwhile the ascendancy of what has been called the neo-conservative movement—intellectuals who had become prominent during the Reagan period but who were in many cases former left-wing, independent intellectuals like the social commentator Irving Kristol and the philosopher Sidney Hook—brought with it a whole host of new journals advancing an openly reactionary, or at least conservative social agenda (Jacoby mentions the extreme right-wing quarterly *The New Criterion* in particular). These forces, says Jacoby, were and still are much more assiduous at courting young writers, potential intellectual leaders who can take over from the older ranks. Whereas the *New York Review of Books,* the most prestigious intellectually liberal journal in America, had once pioneered daring ideas as expressed by new and radical writers, it had now acquired "a deplorable record" resembling in its aging Anglophilia "Oxford teas rather than New York delis." Jacoby concludes that the *New York Review* "never nurtured or heeded younger American intellectuals. For a quarter century it withdrew from the cultural bank without making any investments. Today the operation must rely on imported intellectual capital, mainly from England." All this is due in part "not to a lockout but to a shutdown of the old urban and cultural centers."[5]

⁵Ibid., pp. 219–20.

Jacoby keeps coming back to his idea of an intellectual, whom he describes as "an incorrigibly independent soul answering to no one." All that we have now, he says, is a missing generation which has been replaced by buttoned-up, impossible to understand classroom technicians, hired by committee, anxious to please various patrons and agencies, bristling with academic credentials and a social authority that does not promote debate but establishes reputations and intimidates nonexperts. This is a very gloomy picture, but is it an accurate one? Is what Jacoby says about the reason for the disappearance of intellectuals true, or can we offer in fact a more accurate diagnosis?

In the first place I think it is wrong to be invidious about the university, or even about the United States. There was a brief period in France shortly after the Second World War when a handful of prominent independent intellectuals like Sartre, Camus, Aron, de Beauvoir, seemed to represent the classical idea—not necessarily the reality—of intellectuals descended from their great (but alas often mythical) nineteenth-century prototypes like Ernest Renan and Wilhelm von Humboldt. But what Jacoby doesn't talk about is that intellectual work in the twentieth century has been centrally concerned not just with public debate and elevated polemic of the sort advocated by Julien Benda and exemplified perhaps by Bertrand Russell and a few Bohemian New York intellectuals, but also with criticism and disenchantment, with the exposure of false prophets and debunking of ancient traditions and hallowed names.

Besides, being an intellectual is not at all inconsistent

with being an academic or a pianist for that matter. The brilliant Canadian pianist Glenn Gould (1932–1982) was a recording artist on contract to large corporations for the whole of his performing life: this did not prevent him from being an iconoclastic reinterpreter of and commentator on classical music with tremendous influence on the way performance is executed and judged. By the same token academic intellectuals—historians, for example—have totally reshaped thought about the writing of history, the stability of traditions, the role of language in society. One thinks of Eric Hobsbawm and E. P. Thompson in England, or Hayden White in America. Their work has had wide diffusion beyond the academy, although it mostly was born and nurtured inside it.

As for the United States being especially guilty of denaturing intellectual life, one would have to dispute that, since everywhere one looks today, even in France, the intellectual is no longer a Bohemian or a café-philosopher, but has become a quite different figure, representing many different kinds of concerns, making his or her representations in a very different, dramatically altered way. As I have been suggesting throughout these lectures, the intellectual does not represent a statuelike icon, but an individual vocation, an energy, a stubborn force engaging as a committed and recognizable voice in language and in society with a whole slew of issues, all of them having to do in the end with a combination of enlightenment and emancipation or freedom. The particular threat to the intellectual today, whether in the West or the non-Western world, is not the academy, nor the suburbs, nor the appalling commercialism of journalism and publishing houses, but rather an attitude that I will call professionalism. By professionalism I mean thinking of your work as an intellectual as something you do for a living, between the hours of nine and five with one eye on the clock, and another cocked at what is considered to be proper, professional behavior—not rocking the boat, not straying outside the accepted paradigms or limits, making yourself marketable and above all presentable, hence uncontroversial and unpolitical and "objective."

Let us return to Sartre. At the very moment that he seems to be advocating the idea that man (no mention of woman) is free to choose his own destiny, he also says that the situation—one of Sartre's favorite words—may prevent the full exercise of such freedom. And yet, Sartre adds, it is wrong to say that milieu and situation unilaterally determine the writer or intellectual: rather there is a constant movement back and forth between them. In his credo as an intellectual published in 1947, *What Is Literature?*, Sartre uses the word *writer* rather than intellectual, but it is clear that he is speaking about the role of the intellectual in society, as in the following (all-male) passage:

I am an author, first of all, by my free intention to write. But at once it follows that I become a man whom other men consider as a writer, that is, who has to respond to a certain demand and who has been invested with a certain social function. Whatever game he may want to play, he must play it on the basis of the representation which others have of him. He may want to modify the character that one attributes to the man of letters [or intellectual] in a given society; but in order to change it, he must first slip into it. Hence, the public intervenes, with its customs, its vision of the world, and its conception of society and of literature within that society. It surrounds the writer, it hems him in, and its imperious or sly demands, its refusals and its flights, are the given facts on whose basis a work can be constructed.[6]

Sartre is not saying that the intellectual is a kind of withdrawn philosopher-king whom one ought to idealize and venerate as such. On the contrary—and this is something that contemporary lamenters over the disappearance of intellectuals tend to miss—the intellectual is constantly subject not only to the demands of his or her society but also to quite substantial modifications in the status of intellectuals as members of a distinct group. In assuming that the intellectual ought to have sovereignty, or a kind of unrestricted authority over moral and mental life in a society, critics of the contemporary scene simply refuse to see how much energy has been poured into resisting, even attacking, authority of late, with the radical changes in the intellectual's self-representation that has been produced.

Today's society still hems in and surrounds the writer, sometimes with prizes and rewards, often with denigration or ridiculing of intellectual work altogether, still more often with saying that the true intellectual ought to be only

[6]Jean-Paul Sartre, *What Is Literature? And Other Essays* (Cambridge, Mass.: Harvard University Press, 1988), pp. 77–78.

an expert professional in his or her field. I don't recall
Sartre ever saying that the intellectual should remain outside the university necessarily: he *did* say that the intellectual is never more an intellectual than when surrounded,
cajoled, hemmed in, hectored by society to be one thing
or another, because only then and on that basis can intellectual work be constructed. When he refused the Nobel
Prize in 1964 he was acting precisely according to his
principles.

What are these pressures today? And how do they fit
what I have been calling professionalism? What I want to
discuss are four pressures which I believe challenge the
intellectual's ingenuity and will. None of them is unique
to only one society. Despite their pervasiveness, each of
them can be countered by what I shall call amateurism,
the desire to be moved not by profit or reward but by love
for and unquenchable interest in the larger picture, in making connections across lines and barriers, in refusing to be
tied down to a specialty, in caring for ideas and values despite the restrictions of a profession.

Specialization is the first of these pressures. The
higher one goes in the education system today, the more
one is limited to a relatively narrow area of knowledge.
Now no one can have anything against competence as such,
but when it involves losing sight of anything outside one's
immediate field—say, early Victorian love poetry—and the
sacrifice of one's general culture to a set of authorities and
canonical ideas, then competence of that sort is not worth
the price paid for it.

In the study of literature, for example, which is my

particular interest, specialization has meant an increasing technical formalism, and less and less of a historical sense of what real experiences actually went into the making of a work of literature. Specialization means losing sight of the raw effort of constructing either art or knowledge; as a result you cannot view knowledge and art as choices and decisions, commitments and alignments, but only in terms of impersonal theories or methodologies. To be a specialist in literature too often means shutting out history or music, or politics. In the end as a fully specialized literary intellectual you become tame and accepting of whatever the so-called leaders in the field will allow. Specialization also kills your sense of excitement and discovery, both of which are irreducibly present in the intellectual's makeup. In the final analysis, giving up to specialization is, I have always felt, laziness, so you end up doing what others tell you, because that is your specialty after all.

If specialization is a kind of general instrumental pressure present in all systems of education everywhere, expertise and the cult of the certified expert are more particular pressures in the postwar world. To be an expert you have to be certified by the proper authorities; they instruct you in speaking the right language, citing the right authorities, holding down the right territory. This is especially true when sensitive and/or profitable areas of knowledge are at stake. There has been a great deal of discussion recently of something called "political correctness," an insidious phrase applied to academic humanists who, it is frequently said, do not think independently but rather according to norms established by a cabal of leftists;

these norms are supposed to be overly sensitive to racism, sexism, and the like, instead of allowing people to debate in what is supposed to be an "open" manner.

The truth is that the campaign against political correctness has mainly been conducted by various conservatives and other champions of family values. Although some of the things they say have some merit—especially when they pick up on the sheer mindlessness of unthinking cant—their campaign totally overlooks the amazing conformity and political correctness where, for example, military, national security, foreign and economic policy have been concerned. During the immediate postwar years, for example, so far as the Soviet Union was concerned you were required to accept unquestioningly the premises of the Cold War, the total evil of the Soviet Union, and so on and so forth. For an even longer period of time, roughly from the mid-1940s until the mid-1970s, the official American idea held that freedom in the Third World meant simply freedom from communism: it reigned virtually unchallenged; and with it went the notion endlessly elaborated by legions of sociologists, anthropologists, political scientists and economists, that "development" was non-ideological, derived from the West, and involved economic takeoff, modernization, anticommunism, and a devotion among some political leaders to formal alliances with the United States.

For the United States and some of its allies like Britain and France, these views about defense and security often meant pursuing imperial policies, in which counterinsurgency and an implacable opposition to native nationalism (always seen as tending towards communism and the Soviet Union) brought immense disasters in the form of costly wars and invasions (like Vietnam), indirect support for invasions and massacres (like those undertaken by allies of the West such as Indonesia, El Salvador, and Israel), client regimes with grotesquely distorted economies. To disagree with all this meant, in effect, interfering with a controlled market for expertise tailored to further the national effort. If, for instance, you were not a political scientist trained in the American university system with a healthy respect for development theory and national security, you were not listened to, in some cases not allowed to speak, but challenged on the basis of your nonexpertise.

For "expertise" in the end has rather little, strictly speaking, to do with knowledge. Some of the material brought to bear on the Vietnamese war by Noam Chomsky is far greater in scope and accuracy than similar writing by certified experts. But whereas Chomsky moved beyond the ritually patriotic notions—that included the idea that "we" were coming to the aid of our allies, or that "we" were defending freedom against a Moscow or Peking-inspired takeover—and took on the real motives that governed U.S. behavior, the certified experts, who wanted to be asked back to consult or speak at the State Department or work for the Rand Corporation, never strayed into that territory at all. Chomsky has told the story of how as a linguist he has been invited by mathematicians to speak about his theories, and is usually met with respectful interest, despite his relative ignorance of mathematical lingo. Yet when he tries to represent U.S. foreign policy from

an adversarial standpoint, the recognized experts on foreign policy try to prevent his speaking on the basis of his
lack of certification as a foreign policy expert. There is
little refutation offered his arguments; just the statement
that he stands outside acceptable debate or consensus.

The third pressure of professionalism is the inevitable
drift towards power and authority in its adherents, towards
the requirements and prerogatives of power, and towards
being directly employed by it. In the United States the
extent to which the agenda of the national security deter-
mined priorities and the mentality of academic research
during the period when the U.S. was competing with the
Soviet Union for world hegemony is quite staggering. A
similar situation obtained in the Soviet Union, but in the
West no one had any illusions about free inquiry *there*. We
are only just beginning to wake up to what it meant—that
the American Departments of State and Defence provided
more money than any other single donor for university
research in science and technology: this was preeminently
true of MIT and Stanford, who between them received
the biggest amounts for decades.

But it was also the case that during the same period
university social science and even humanities departments
were funded by the government for the same general
agenda. Something like this occurs in all societies of course,
but it was noteworthy in the U.S. because in the case of
some of the anti-guerrilla research carried out in support
of policy in the Third World—in Southeast Asia, Latin
America, and the Middle East principally—the research
was applied directly in covert activities, sabotage, and even

outright war. Questions of morality and justice were de-
ferred so that contracts—such as the notorious Project
Camelot undertaken by social scientists for the Army beginning in 1964, in order to study not only the breakdown
of various societies all over the world, but also how to
prevent the breakdown from occurring—could be fulfilled.

Nor has this been all. Centralizing powers in American
civil society such as the Republican or Democratic
parties; industry or special interest lobbies like those
created or maintained by the gun-manufacturing, oil, and
tobacco corporations; large foundations like those
established by the Rockefellers, the Fords, or the Mel-
lons—all employ academic experts to carry out research
and study programs that further commercial as well as political agendas. This of course is part of what is considered
normal behavior in a free market system, and occurs
throughout Europe and the Far East as well. There are
grants and fellowships to be had from think tanks, plus
sabbatical leaves and publishing subventions, as well as
professional advancement and recognition.

Everything about the system is aboveboard and, as I
have said, is acceptable according to the standards of competition and market response that govern behavior under
advanced capitalism in a liberal and democratic society. But
in spending a lot of time worrying about the restrictions
on thought and intellectual freedom under totalitarian systems of government we have not been as fastidious in
considering the threats to the individual intellectual of a
system that rewards intellectual conformity, as well as willing participation in goals that have been set not by science

but by the government; accordingly, research and accreditation are controlled in order to get and keep a larger share of the market.

In other words, the space for individual and subjective intellectual representation, for asking questions and challenging the wisdom of a war or an immense social program that awards contracts and endows prizes, has shrunk dramatically from what it was a hundred years ago when Stephen Dedalus could say that as an intellectual his duty was not to serve any power or authority at all. Now I do not want to suggest as some have—rather sentimentally I think—that we should recover a time when universities weren't so big, and the opportunities they now offer were not so lavish. To my mind the Western university, certainly in America, still can offer the intellectual a quasi-utopian space in which reflection and research can go on, albeit under new constraints and pressures.

Therefore, the problem for the intellectual is to try to deal with the impingements of modern professionalization as I have been discussing them, not by pretending that they are not there, or denying their influence, but by representing a different set of values and prerogatives. These I shall collect under the name of *amateurism,* literally, an activity that is fueled by care and affection rather than by profit and selfish, narrow specialization.

The intellectual today ought to be an amateur, someone who considers that to be a thinking and concerned member of a society one is entitled to raise moral issues at the heart of even the most technical and professionalized activity as it involves one's country, its power, its mode of interacting with its citizens as well as with other societies. In addition, the intellectual's spirit as an amateur can enter and transform the merely professional routine most of us go through into something much more lively and radical; instead of doing what one is supposed to do one can ask why one does it, who benefits from it, how can it reconnect with a personal project and original thoughts.

Every intellectual has an audience and a constituency. The issue is whether that audience is there to be satisfied, and hence a client to be kept happy, or whether it is there to be challenged, and hence stirred into outright opposition or mobilized into greater democratic participation in the society. But in either case, there is no getting around authority and power, and no getting around the intellectual's relationship to them. How does the intellectual address authority: as a professional supplicant or as its unrewarded, amateurish conscience?

V

Speaking Truth to Power

I WANT TO continue to look at specialization and professionalism, and how the intellectual confronts the question
of power and authority. During the mid-1960s just a short
while before opposition to the Vietnamese war became
very vocal and widespread, I was approached by an older-
looking undergraduate student at Columbia for admission
to a seminar with limited enrollment. Part of his line to
me was that he was a veteran of the war, having served
there in the air force. As we chatted, he provided me with
a fascinatingly eerie glimpse into the mentality of the
professional—in this case a seasoned pilot—whose vocabulary for his work could be described as "Insidese." I shall
never forget the shock I received when in responding to
my insistent question, "What did you actually do in the air
force?" he replied, "Target acquisition." It took me several
more minutes to figure out that he was a bombardier whose
job it was, well, to bomb, but he had coated it in a professional language that in a certain sense was meant to exclude

and mystify the rather more direct probings of a rank outsider. I did take him into the seminar, by the way—perhaps because I thought I could keep an eye on him and, as an added inducement, persuade him to drop the appalling jargon. "Target acquisition" indeed.

In a more consistent and sustained way, I think, intellectuals who are close to policy formulation and can control patronage of the kind that gives or withholds jobs, stipends, promotions tend to watch out for individuals who do not toe the line professionally and in the eyes of their superiors gradually come to exude an air of controversy and noncooperation. Understandably of course, if you want a job done—let us say that you and your team have to provide the State Department or Foreign Office with a policy paper on Bosnia by next week—you need to surround yourself with people who are loyal, share the same assumptions, speak the same language. I have always felt that for an intellectual who represents the kinds of things I have been discussing in these lectures, being in that sort of professional position, where you are principally serving and winning rewards from power, is not at all conducive to the exercise of that critical and relatively independent spirit of analysis and judgment that, from my point of view, ought to be the intellectual's contribution. In other words, the intellectual, properly speaking, is not a functionary or an employee completely given up to the policy goals of a government or a large corporation, or even a guild of like-minded professionals. In such situations the temptations to turn off one's moral sense, or to think entirely from within the specialty, or to curtail skepticism in favor of conformity are far too great to be trusted. Many intellectuals succumb completely to these temptations, and to some degree all of us do. No one is totally self-supporting, not even the greatest of free spirits.

I have already suggested that as a way of maintaining relative intellectual independence, having the attitude of an amateur instead of a professional is a better course. But let me be practical and personal for a moment. In the first place amateurism means choosing the risks and uncertain results of the public sphere—a lecture or a book or an article in wide and unrestricted circulation—over the insider space controlled by experts and professionals. Several times over the past two years I have been asked by the media to be a paid consultant. This I have refused to do, simply because it meant being confined to one television station or journal, and confined also to the going political language and conceptual framework of that outlet. Similarly I have never had any interest in paid consultancies to or for the government, where you would have no idea of what use your ideas might later be put to. Secondly, delivering knowledge directly for a fee is very different if, on the one hand, a university asks you to give a public lecture or if, on the other, you are asked to speak only to a small and closed circle of officials. That seems very obvious to me, so I have always welcomed university lectures and always turned down the others. And, thirdly, to get more political, whenever I have been asked for help by a Palestinian group, or by a South African university to visit and to speak against apartheid and for academic freedom, I have routinely accepted.

In the end, I am moved by causes and ideas that I can actually choose to support because they conform to values and principles that I believe in. I do not therefore consider myself bound by my professional training in literature, consequently ruling myself out from matters of public policy just because I am only certified to teach modern European and American literature. I speak and write about broader matters because as a rank amateur I am spurred on by commitments that go well beyond my narrow professional career. Of course I make a conscious effort to acquire a new and wider audience for these views, which I never present inside a classroom.

But what are these amateur forays into the public sphere really about? Is the intellectual galvanized into intellectual action by primordial, local, instinctive loyalties—one's race, or people, or religion—or is there some more universal and rational set of principles that can and perhaps do govern how one speaks and writes? In effect I am asking *the* basic question for the intellectual: how does one speak the truth? What truth? For whom and where?

Unfortunately we must begin to respond by saying that there is no system or method that is broad and certain enough to provide the intellectual with direct answers to these questions. In the secular world—our world, the historical and social world made by human effort—the intellectual has only secular means to work with; revelation and inspiration, while perfectly feasible as modes for understanding in private life, are disasters and even barbaric when put to use by theoretically minded men and women. Indeed I would go so far as saying that the intellectual must

be involved in a lifelong dispute with all the guardians of sacred vision or text, whose depredations are legion and whose heavy hand brooks no disagreement and certainly no diversity. Uncompromising freedom of opinion and expression is the secular intellectual's main bastion: to abandon its defense or to tolerate tamperings with any of its foundations is in effect to betray the intellectual's calling. That is why the defense of Salman Rushdie's *Satanic Verses* has been so absolutely central an issue, both for its own sake and for the sake of every other infringement against the right to expression of journalists, novelists, essayists, poets, historians.

And this is not just an issue for those in the Islamic world, but also in the Jewish and Christian worlds too. Freedom of expression cannot be sought invidiously in one territory and ignored in another. For with authorities who claim the secular right to defend divine decree there can be no debate no matter where they are, whereas for the intellectual, tough searching debate is the core of activity, the very stage and setting of what intellectuals without revelation really do. But we are back to square one: what truth and principles should one defend, uphold, represent? This is no Pontius Pilate's question, a way of washing one's hands of a difficult case, but the necessary beginning of a survey of where today the intellectual stands and what a treacherous, uncharted minefield surrounds him or her.

Take as a starting point the whole, by now extremely disputatious matter of objectivity, or accuracy, or facts. In 1988 the American historian Peter Novick published a massive volume whose title dramatized the quandary with exemplary efficiency. It was called *That Noble Dream,* and subtitled *The "Objectivity Question" and the American Historical Professor.* Drawing on materials taken from a century of historiographic enterprise in the United States, Novick showed how the very nub of historical investigation—the ideal of objectivity by which a historian seizes the opportunity to render facts as realistically and accurately as possible—gradually evolved into a quagmire of competing claims and counterclaims, all of them wearing down any semblance of agreement by historians as to what objectivity was to the merest fig leaf, and often not even to that. Objectivity has had to do service in wartime as "our," that is American as opposed to fascist German, truth; in peacetime as the objective truth of each competing separate group—women, African-Americans, Asian-Americans, gays, white men, and on and on—and each school (Marxist, establishment, deconstructionist, cultural). After such a babble of knowledges what possible convergence could there be, Novick asks, and he concludes mournfully that "as a broad community of discourse, as a community of scholars united by common aims, common standards, and common purposes, the discipline of history had ceased to exist. . . . The professor [of history] was as described in the last verse of the Book of Judges: In those days there was no king in Israel; every man did that which was right in his own eyes."[1]

---

[1]Peter Novick, *That Noble Dream: The "Objectivity Question" and the American Historical Profession* (Cambridge: Cambridge University Press, 1988), p. 628.

As I mentioned in my last lecture, one of the main intellectual activities of our century has been the questioning, not to say undermining, of authority. So to add to Novick's findings we would have to say that not only did a consensus disappear on what constituted objective reality, but a lot of traditional authorities, including God, were in the main swept away. There has even been an influential school of philosophers, among whom Michel Foucault ranks very high, who say that to speak of an author at all (as in "the author of Milton's poems") is a highly tendentious, not to say ideological, overstatement.

In the face of this quite formidable onslaught, to regress either into hand-wringing impotence or into muscular reassertions of traditional values, as characterized by the global neo-conservative movement, will not do. I think it is true to say that the critique of objectivity and authority did perform a positive service by underlining how, in the secular world, human beings construct their truths, and that, for example, the so-called objective truth of the white man's superiority built and maintained by the classical European colonial empires also rested on a violent subjugation of African and Asian peoples, who, it is equally true, fought that particular imposed "truth" in order to provide an independent order of their own. And so now everyone comes forward with new and often violently opposed views of the world: one hears endless talk about Judeo-Christian values, Afrocentric values, Muslim truths, Eastern truths, Western truths, each providing a complete program for excluding all the others. There is now more intolerance and strident assertiveness abroad everywhere than any one system can handle.

The result is an almost complete absence of universals, even though very often the rhetoric suggests, for instance, that "our" values (whatever those may happen to be) are in fact universal. One of the shabbiest of all intellectual gambits is to pontificate about abuses in someone else's society and to excuse exactly the same practices in one's own. For me the classic example of this is provided by the brilliant nineteenth-century French intellectual Alexis de Tocqueville, who, to many of us educated to believe in classical liberal and Western democratic values, exemplified those values almost to the letter. Having written his assessment of democracy in America and having criticized American mistreatment of Indians and black slaves, Tocqueville later had to deal with French colonial policies in Algeria during the late 1830s and 1840s, where under Marshall Bugeaud the French army of occupation undertook a savage war of pacification against the Algerian Muslims. All of a sudden, as one reads Tocqueville on Algeria, the very norms with which he had humanely demurred at American malfeasance are suspended for French actions. Not that he does not cite reasons: he does, but they are lame extenuations whose purpose is to license French colonialism in the name of what he calls national pride. Massacres leave him unmoved; Muslims, he says, belong to an inferior religion and must be disciplined. In short, the apparent universalism of his language for America is denied, willfully denied application to his own country, even as his own country, France, pursues similarly inhumane policies.[2]

It must be added, however, that Tocqueville (and John Stuart Mill for that matter, whose commendable ideas about democratic freedoms in England he said did not apply to India) lived during a period when the ideas of a universal norm of international behavior meant in effect the right of European power and European representations of other people to hold sway, so nugatory and secondary did the nonwhite peoples of the world seem. Besides, according to nineteenth-century Westerners, there were no independent African or Asian peoples of consequence to challenge the draconian brutality of laws that were applied unilaterally by colonial armies to black- or brown-skinned races. Their destiny was to be ruled. Frantz Fanon, Aimé Césaire, and C. L. R. James—to mention three great anti-imperialist black intellectuals—did not live and write until the twentieth century, so what they and the liberation movements of which they were a part accomplished culturally and politically in establishing the right of colonized peoples to equal treatment was not available to Tocqueville or Mill. But these changed perspectives are available to contemporary intellectuals who have not often drawn the inevitable conclusions, that if you wish to uphold basic human justice you must do so for everyone, not just selectively for the people that your side, your culture, your nation designates as okay.

[2]I have discussed the imperial context of this in detail in *Culture and Imperialism* (New York: Alfred A. Knopf, 1993), pp. 169–90.

The fundamental problem is therefore how to reconcile one's identity and the actualities of one's own culture, society, and history to the reality of other identities,
cultures, peoples. This can never be done simply by asserting one's preference for what is already one's own: tubthumping about the glories of "our" culture or the
triumphs of "our" history is not worthy of the intellectual's
energy, especially not today when so many societies are
comprised of different races and backgrounds as to resist
any reductive formulas. As I have tried to show here, the
public realm in which intellectuals make their representations is extremely complex and contains uncomfortable
features, but the meaning of an effective intervention in
that realm has to rest on the intellectual's unbudgeable
conviction in a concept of justice and fairness that allows
for differences between nations and individuals, without
at the same time assigning them to hidden hierarchies,
preferences, evaluations. Everyone today professes a liberal language of equality and harmony for all. The problem
for the intellectual is to bring these notions to bear on
actual situations where the gap between the profession of
equality and justice, on the one hand, and the rather less
edifying reality, on the other, is very great.

This is most easily demonstrated in international relations, which is the reason I have stressed them so much
in these lectures. A couple of recent examples illustrate
what I have in mind. During the period just after Iraq's
illegal invasion of Kuwait public discussion in the West
justly focused on the unacceptability of the aggression
which with extreme brutality sought to eliminate Kuwaiti

existence. And as it became clear that the American intention was in fact to use military force against Iraq, the public rhetoric encouraged processes at the United Nations that would ensure the passage of resolutions—based on the UN charter—demanding sanctions and the possible use of force against Iraq. Of the few intellectuals who opposed both the Iraqi invasion and the subsequent use of largely American force in Operation Desert Storm, none to my knowledge cited any evidence or made any attempt actually to excuse Iraq for its invasion.

But what was correctly remarked at the time was how considerably weakened the American case against Iraq became when the Bush administration with its enormous power pressed the UN forward towards war, ignoring the numerous possibilities of a negotiated reversal of the occupation before January 15 when the counteroffensive began, and refused to discuss other UN resolutions on other illegal occupations and invasions of territory that had involved the United States itself or some of its close allies. Of course the real issue in the Gulf so far as the U.S. was concerned was oil and strategic power, not the Bush administration's professed principles, but what compromised intellectual discussion throughout the country, in its reiterations of the inadmissibility of land unilaterally acquired by force, was the absence of universal application of the idea. What never seemed relevant to the many American intellectuals who supported the war was that the U.S. itself had just recently invaded and for a time occupied the sovereign state of Panama. Surely if one criticized Iraq, it therefore followed that the U.S. deserved the same criticism? But no: "our" motives were higher, Saddam was a Hitler, whereas "we" were moved by largely altruistic and disinterested motives, and therefore this was a just war.

Or consider the Soviet invasion of Afghanistan, equally wrong and equally condemnable. But U.S. allies such as Israel and Turkey had illegally occupied territories before the Russians moved into Afghanistan. Similarly, another U.S. ally, Indonesia, massacred literally hundreds of thousands of Timorese in an illegal invasion during the middle 1970s; there is evidence to show that the U.S. knew about and supported the horrors of the East Timor war, but few intellectuals in the U.S., busy as always with the crimes of the Soviet Union, said much about that.[3] And looming back in time was the enormous American invasion of Indochina, with results in sheer destructiveness wreaked on small, mainly peasant societies that are staggering. The principle here seems to have been that professional experts on U.S. foreign and military policy should confine their attention to winning a war against the other superpower and its surrogates in Vietnam or Afghanistan, and our own misdeeds be damned. Such are the ways of *realpolitik*.

Certainly they are, but my point would be that for the contemporary intellectual living at a time that is already confused by the disappearance of what seem to have been objective moral norms and sensible authority, is it accept-

[3]For an account of these dubious intellectual procedures, see Noam Chomsky, *Necessary Illusions: Thought Control in Democratic Societies* (Boston: South End Press, 1989).

able simply either blindly to support the behavior of one's own country and overlook its crimes or to say rather supinely, "I believe they all do it, and that's the way of the world"? What we must be able to say instead is that intellectuals are not professionals denatured by their fawning service to an extremely flawed power, but—to repeat—are *intellectuals* with an alternative and more principled stand that enables them in effect to speak the truth to power.

By that I do not mean here some Old Testament-like thunderings, proclaiming everyone to be sinful and basically evil. I mean something much more modest and a great deal more effective. To speak of consistency in upholding standards of international behavior and the support of human rights is not to look inwards for a guiding light supplied to one by inspiration or prophetic intuition. Most, if not all, countries in the world are signatories to a Universal Declaration of Human Rights, adopted and proclaimed in 1948, reaffirmed by every new member state of the UN. There are equally solemn conventions on the rules of war, on treatment of prisoners, on the rights of workers, women, children, immigrants and refugees. None of these documents says anything about *disqualified* or less equal races or peoples. All are entitled to the same freedoms.[4] Of course these rights are violated on a daily basis, as the genocide in Bosnia today bears witness. For an

[4]A fuller version of this argument is to be found in my "Nationalism, Human Rights, and Interpretation" in *Freedom and Interpretation: The Oxford Amnesty Lectures, 1992,* ed. Barbara Johnson (New York: Basic Books, 1993), pp. 175–205.

American or Egyptian or Chinese government official these rights are at best looked at "practically," not consistently. But such are the norms of power, which are precisely not those of the intellectual, whose role is at very least to apply the same standards and norms of behavior now already collectively accepted on paper by the entire international community.

Of course there are questions of patriotism and loyalty to one's people. And of course the intellectual is not an uncomplicated automaton, hurling mathematically devised laws and rules across the board. And of course fear and the normal limitations on one's time and attention and capacity as an individual voice operate with fearsome efficiency. But whereas we are right to bewail the disappearance of a consensus on what constitutes objectivity, we are not by the same token completely adrift in self-indulgent subjectivity. Taking refuge inside a profession or nationality (I have already said) is only taking refuge; it is not answer to the goads all of us receive just by reading the morning's news.

No one can speak up all the time on all the issues. But, I believe, there is a special duty to address the constituted and authorized powers of one's own society, which are accountable to its citizenry, particularly when those powers are exercised in a manifestly disproportionate and immoral war, or in a deliberate program of discrimination, repression, and collective cruelty. As I said in my second lecture, all of us live inside national borders, we use national languages, we address (most of the time) our national communities. For an intellectual who lives in America, there is a reality to be faced, namely that our country is first of all an extremely diverse immigrant society, with fantastic resources and accomplishments, but it also contains a redoubtable set of internal inequities and external interventions that cannot be ignored. While I cannot speak for intellectuals elsewhere, surely the basic point remains pertinent, with the difference that in other countries the state in question is not a global power like the United States.

In all these instances, the intellectual meaning of a situation is arrived at by comparing the known and available facts with a norm, also known and available. This is not an easy task, since documentation, research, probings are required in order to get beyond the usually piecemeal, fragmentary and necessarily flawed way in which information is presented. But in most cases it is possible, I believe, to ascertain whether in fact a massacre was committed or an official cover-up produced. The first imperative is to find out what occurred and then why, not as isolated events but as part of an unfolding history whose broad contours include one's own nation as an actor. The incoherence of the standard foreign policy analysis performed by apologists, strategists and planners is that it concentrates on others as the objects of a situation, rarely on "our" involvement and what it wrought. Even more rarely is it compared to a moral norm.

The goal of speaking the truth is, in so administered a mass society as ours, mainly to project a better state of affairs and one that corresponds more closely to a set of moral principles—peace, reconciliation, abatement of suffering—applied to the known facts. This has been called *abduction* by the American pragmatist philosopher C. S. Peirce, and has been used effectively by the celebrated contemporary intellectual Noam Chomsky.[5] Certainly in writing and speaking, one's aim is not to show everyone how right one is but rather to try to induce a change in the moral climate whereby aggression is seen as such, the unjust punishment of peoples or individuals is either prevented or given up, the recognition of rights and democratic freedoms is established as a norm for everyone, not invidiously for a select few. Admittedly, however, these are idealistic and often unrealizable aims; and in a sense they are not as immediately relevant to my subject here as the intellectual's individual performance, as I have been saying, when more often than not the tendency is to back away or simply to toe the line.

Nothing in my view is more reprehensible than those habits of mind in the intellectual that induce avoidance, that characteristic turning away from a difficult and principled position which you know to be the right one, but which you decide not to take. You do not want to appear too political; you are afraid of seeming controversial; you need the approval of a boss or an authority figure; you want to keep a reputation for being balanced, objective, moderate; your hope is to be asked back, to consult, to be on a board or prestigious committee, and so to remain within the responsible mainstream; someday you hope to

[5]Noam Chomsky, *Language and Mind* (New York: Harcourt Brace Jovanovich, 1972), pp. 90–99.

get an honorary degree, a big prize, perhaps even an ambassadorship.

For an intellectual these habits of mind are corrupting *par excellence*. If anything can denature, neutralize, and finally kill a passionate intellectual life it is the internalization of such habits. Personally I have encountered them in one of the toughest of all contemporary issues, Palestine, where fear of speaking out about one of the greatest injustices in modern history has hobbled, blinkered, muzzled many who know the truth and are in a position to serve it. For despite the abuse and vilification that any outspoken supporter of Palestinian rights and self-determination earns for him or herself, the truth deserves to be spoken, represented by an unafraid and compassionate intellectual. This has been even more true as a result of the Oslo Declaration of Principles signed on September 13, 1993, between the PLO and Israel. The great euphoria produced by this extremely limited breakthrough obscured the fact that far from guaranteeing Palestinian rights, the document in effect guaranteed the prolongation of Israeli control over the Occupied Territories. To criticize this meant in effect taking a position against "hope" and "peace."[6]

And finally a word about the mode of intellectual intervention. The intellectual does not climb a mountain or pulpit and declaim from the heights. Obviously you want to speak your piece where it can be heard best; and also you want it represented in such a way as to influence with

[6]See my article "The Morning After," *London Review of Books*, 21 October 1993, volume 15, no. 20, 3–5.

an ongoing and actual process, for instance, the cause of peace and justice. Yes, the intellectual's voice is lonely, but it has resonance only because it associates itself freely with the reality of a movement, the aspirations of a people, the common pursuit of a shared ideal. Opportunism dictates that in the West, much given to full-scale critiques of, for instance, Palestinian terror or immoderation, you denounce them soundly, and then go on to praise Israeli democracy. Then you must say something good about peace. Intellectual responsibility of course dictates that you must say all those things to Palestinians, but that you make your main point in New York, in Paris, in London around the issue which in those places you can most affect, by promoting the idea of Palestinian freedom and the freedom from terror and extremism of *all* concerned, not just the weakest and most easily bashed party.

Speaking the truth to power is no Panglossian idealism: it is carefully weighing the alternatives, picking the right one, and then intelligently representing it where it can do the most good and cause the right change.

VI

Gods That Always Fail

HE WAS A brilliantly eloquent and charismatic Iranian intellectual whom I was first introduced to in the West sometime in 1978. A writer and teacher of considerable accomplishment and learning, he played a significant role in spreading knowledge of the Shah's unpopular rule, and later that same year of the new figures who were soon to come to power in Teheran. He spoke respectfully of Imam Khomeini at the time, and was soon to become visibly associated with the relatively young men around Khomeini who were of course Muslim but assuredly not militant Islamists, men like Abol Hassan Bani Sadr and Sadek Ghotbzadeh.

A few weeks after the Islamic revolution of Iran had consolidated power inside the country, my acquaintance (who had gone back to Iran for the new government's installation) returned to the West as an ambassador to an important metropolitan center. I recall attending and once or twice participating with him on panels on the Middle

East after the Shah's fall. I saw him during the time of the very long hostage crisis, as it was called in America, and he regularly expressed anguish and even anger at the ruffians who had engineered the embassy takeover and the subsequent holding of fifty or so civilian hostages. The unmistakable impression I had of him was of a decent man who had committed himself to the new order, and had gone as far as defending and even serving it as a loyal emissary abroad. I knew him as an observant Muslim but by no means a fanatic. He was skillful at fending off skepticism and attacks on his government; this he did, I thought, with conviction and appropriate discrimination, but he left no one in doubt—certainly not me at any rate—that although he disagreed with some of his colleagues in the Iranian government, and that he saw things at this level as very much in flux, Imam Khomeini was, and ought to have been, *the* authority in Iran. He was such a loyalist that once when he came to Beirut he told me that he had refused to shake hands with a Palestinian leader (this was when the PLO and the Islamic Revolution were allies) because "he had criticized the Imam."

I think it must have been a few months before the hostages were released in early 1981 that he resigned his ambassadorial post and returned to Iran, this time as special assistant to President Bani Sadr. The antagonistic lines between President and Imam, however, were already well drawn, and of course the President lost. Shortly after he was sacked or deposed by Khomeini, Bani Sadr went into exile and my friend did too, although he had a difficult time actually getting out of Iran. A year or so later he had become a vociferous public critic of Khomeini's Iran, attacking the government and the man he had once served on the very same platforms in New York and London from which he had once defended them both. He had not lost his critical sense of the American role, however, and consistently spoke about United States imperialism: his earlier memories of the Shah's regime and American support for it were seared into his being.

I therefore felt an even greater sadness when a few months after the Gulf War in 1991 I heard him speak about the war, this time as a defender of the American war against Iraq. Like a number of European Left intellectuals he said that in a conflict between imperialism and fascism one should always pick imperialism. I was surprised that none of the formulators of this, in my opinion, unnecessarily attenuated pair of choices had grasped that it would have been quite possible and indeed desirable on both intellectual and political grounds to reject both fascism and imperialism.

In any event, this little story encapsulates one of the dilemmas facing a contemporary intellectual whose interest in what I have been calling the public sphere is not merely theoretical or academic but also involves direct participation. How far should an intellectual go in getting involved? Should one join a party, serve an idea as it is embodied in actual political processes, personalities, jobs, and therefore become a true believer? Or, on the other hand, is there some more discreet—but no less serious and involved—way of joining up without suffering the pain of later betrayal and disillusionment? How far should one's loyalty to a cause take one in being consistently faithful to it? Can one retain independence of mind and, at the same time, *not* go through the agonies of public recantation and confession?

It is not completely coincidental that the story of my Iranian friend's pilgrimage back to Islamic theocracy and out of it is about a quasi-religious conversion, followed by what appeared to be a very dramatic reversal in belief, and a counterconversion. For whether I saw him as an advocate of Islamic revolution and subsequently as an intellectual soldier in its ranks or as an outspoken critic, someone who had left it in an almost shattered disgust, I never doubted my friend's sincerity. He was as fully convincing in the first as he was in the second role—passionate, fluent, blazingly effective as a debater.

I shouldn't here pretend that I was a detached outsider throughout my friend's ordeal. As supporters of Palestinian nationalism during the seventies he and I made common cause against the ponderously interfering role played by the United States, which to our way of thinking propped up the Shah and placated and supported Israel unjustly and anachronistically. We saw both our peoples as victims of cruelly insensitive policies: suppression, dispossession, impoverishment. We were both exiles, of course, although I must confess that even then I had resigned myself to remaining one for the rest of my life. When my friend's team won, so to speak, I was jubilant, and not only because at last he could go home. Ever since the Arab defeat of 1967 the successful Iranian revolution—which was made by an improbable alliance of clergy and common people that had completely confounded even the most sophisticated Marxist Middle East experts—was the first major blow to Western hegemony in the region. Both of us saw it as a victory.

Yet for me as a perhaps stupidly stubborn secular intellectual, I was never particularly taken with Khomeini himself, even before he revealed his darkly tyrannical and unyielding personality as supreme ruler. Not being a joiner or party member by nature, I had never formally enlisted in service. I had certainly become used to being peripheral, outside the circle of power, and perhaps because I had no talent for a position inside that charmed circle, I rationalized the virtues of outsiderhood. I could never completely believe in the men and women—for that is what they were after all, *just* men and women—who commanded forces, led parties and countries, wielded basically unchallenged authority. Hero-worship, and even the notion of heroism itself when applied to most political leaders, has always left me cold. As I watched my friend join, then abandon and then re-join sides, often with great ceremonies of bonding and rejection (such as giving up and then getting back his Western passport), I was strangely glad that being a Palestinian with American citizenship was likely to be my only fate, with no more attractive alternatives to cozy up to, for the rest of my life.

For fourteen years I served as an independent member of the Palestinian parliament in exile, the Palestine National Council, the total number of whose meetings insofar as I attended them at all amounted to about a week altogether. I stayed in the Council as an act of solidarity,

even of defiance, because in the West I felt it was symbolically important to expose oneself as a Palestinian in
that way, as someone who associated himself publicly with
the struggle to resist Israeli policies and to win Palestinian
self-determination. I refused all offers that were made to
me to occupy official positions; I never joined any party
or faction. When during the third year of the *intifada* I
was disturbed by official Palestinian policies in the U.S. I
made my views widely known in Arabic forums. I never
abandoned the struggle, nor obviously did I join the Israeli
or American side, refusing to collaborate with the powers
that I still see as the chief authors of our people's woes.
Similarly I never endorsed the policies of, or even accepted
official invitations from, Arab states.

I am perfectly prepared to admit that these perhaps
too protestant positions of mine are extensions of the essentially impossible and generally losing results of being
Palestinian: we lack territorial sovereignty, and have only
tiny victories and little enough room to celebrate them in.
Perhaps also they rationalize my unwillingness to go as far
as many others have in committing myself completely to
a cause or party, going all the way in conviction and engagement. I simply have not been able to do it, preferring
to retain both the outsider's and the skeptic's autonomy
over the, to me, vaguely religious quality communicated
by the convert's and true believer's enthusiasm. I found
that this sense of critical detachment served me (how well
I am still not completely certain) after the Israel–PLO deal
was announced in August 1993. It seemed to me that the
media-induced euphoria, to say nothing of official decla-

rations of happiness and satisfaction, belied the grim actuality that the PLO leadership had simply surrendered to Israel. To say such things at the time put one in a small minority, but I felt for intellectual and moral reasons it had to be said. Yet the Iranian experiences I have recounted bear some direct comparison with other episodes of conversion and public recantation that dot the twentieth-century intellectual experience, and it is those, both in the Western and Middle Eastern worlds that I know best, that I'd like to consider here.

I do not want to equivocate or allow myself very much ambiguity at the outset: I am against conversion to and belief in a political god of any sort. I consider both as unfitting behavior for the intellectual. This does not mean that the intellectual should remain at the edge of the water, occasionally dipping a toe in, most of the time remaining dry. Everything I have written in these lectures underlines the importance to the intellectual of passionate engagement, risk, exposure, commitment to principles, vulnerability in debating and being involved in worldly causes. For example, the difference I drew earlier between a professional and an amateur intellectual rests precisely on this, that the professional claims detachment on the basis of a profession and pretends to objectivity, whereas the amateur is moved neither by rewards nor by the fulfillment of an immediate career plan but by a committed engagement with ideas and values in the public sphere. The intellectual over time naturally turns towards the political world partly because, unlike the academy or the laboratory, that world is animated by considerations of power and interest writ large that drive a whole society or nation, that, as Marx so fatefully said, take the intellectual from relatively discrete questions of interpretation to much more significant ones of social change and transformation.

Every intellectual whose métier is articulating and representing specific views, ideas, ideologies, logically aspires to making them work in a society. The intellectual who claims to write only for him or herself, or for the sake of pure learning, or abstract science is not to be, and *must not* be, believed. As the great twentieth-century writer Jean Genet once said, the moment you publish essays in a society you have entered political life; so if you want not to be political do not write essays or speak out.

The heart of the conversion phenomenon is joining up, not simply in alignment but in service and, though one hates to use the word, collaboration. There has rarely been a more discrediting and unpleasant instance of this sort of thing in the West generally, and in the United States in particular, than during the Cold War, when legions of intellectuals joined what was considered to be the battle for the hearts and minds of people all over the world. An extremely famous book edited by Richard Crossman in 1949 that epitomized the strangely Manichean aspect of the intellectual Cold War was entitled *The God That Failed;* the phrase and its explicitly religious cachet lived on well past anyone's actual memory of the book's contents, but those do deserve brief summary here.

Intended as a testimonial to the gullibility of prominent Western intellectuals—who included Ignazio Silone,

André Gide, Arthur Koestler, and Stephen Spender among others—*The God That Failed* allowed each of them to recount his experiences of the road to Moscow, the inevitable disenchantment that followed, the subsequent re-embrace of noncommunist faith. Crossman concludes his introduction to the volume by saying in emphatic theological terms: "The Devil once lived in Heaven, and those who have not met him are unlikely to recognize an angel when they see one."[1] This of course is not only politics but a morality play as well. The battle for the intellect has been transformed into a battle for the soul, with implications for intellectual life that have been very baleful. That was certainly the case in the Soviet Union and its satellites, where show trials, mass purges, and a gigantic penitentiary system exemplified the horrors of the ordeal on the other side of the iron curtain.

In the West, many of the former comrades were required often to do public penance, unseemly enough when it involved celebrities like the ones collected in *The God That Failed*, a great deal worse when—in the United States as an especially egregious instance—it induced mass hysteria; and, to someone like myself who came from the Middle East to the U.S. as a schoolboy in the 1950s when McCarthyism was in full course, it shaped a mystifyingly bloody-minded intelligentsia, to this day hung up on a wildly exaggerated internal and external menace. It was all

[1] *The God That Failed,* ed. Richard Crossman (Washington, D.C.: Regnery Gateway, 1987), p. vii.

a dispiritingly self-induced crisis, signifying the triumph of unthinking Manicheanism over rational as well as self-critical analysis.

Whole careers were built not upon intellectual achievement but upon proving the evils of communism, or repentance, or informing on friends or colleagues, or collaborating once again with the enemies of former friends. Whole systems of discourse derived from anti-communism, from the supposed pragmatism of the end of ideology school to its short-lived inheritor in the past few years, the end of history school. Far from being a passive defense of freedom, organized anticommunism in the U.S. led aggressively to covert support by the CIA for otherwise unexceptionable groups such as the Congress of Cultural Freedom—which was involved not only in the worldwide distribution of *The God That Failed* but in subsidizing magazines such as *Encounter*—as well as the infiltration of labor unions, student organizations, churches, and universities.

Obviously many of the successful things done in the name of anticommunism have been chronicled by its supporters as a movement. Other less admirable features are, however, first the corruption of open intellectual discussion and a thriving cultural debate by means of a system of evangelical and finally irrational do's and don'ts (the progenitors of today's "political correctness") and second, certain forms of self-mutilation in public that go on to this day. Both these things have gone side by side with despicable habits of collecting rewards and privileges from one team, only for the same individual to switch sides, then collect rewards from a new patron.

For the time being I want to underline the particularly unpleasant aesthetics of conversion and recantation, how for the individual involved, the public display of assent and subsequent apostasy produces a kind of narcissism and exhibitionism in the intellectual that has lost touch with the people and processes supposedly being served. I have said several times in these lectures that ideally the intellectual represents emancipation and enlightenment, but never as abstractions or as bloodless and distant gods to be served. The intellectual's representations—what he or she represents and how those ideas are represented to an audience—are always tied to and ought to remain an organic part of an ongoing experience in society: of the poor, the disadvantaged, the voiceless, the unrepresented, the powerless. These are equally concrete and ongoing; they cannot survive being transfigured and then frozen into creeds, religious declarations, professional methods.

Such transfigurations sever the living connection between the intellectual and the movement or process of which he or she is a part. Moreover there is the appalling danger of thinking of oneself, one's views, one's rectitude, one's stated positions as all-important. To read over *The God That Failed* testimonial is for me a depressing thing. I want to ask: Why as an intellectual did you believe in a god anyway? And besides, who gave you the right to imagine that your early belief and later disenchantment were so important? In and of itself religious belief is to me both understandable and deeply personal: it is rather when a total dogmatic system in which one side is innocently good, the other irreducibly evil, is substituted for the process, the give-and-take of vital interchange, that the secular intellectual feels the unwelcome and inappropriate encroachment of one realm on another. Politics becomes religious enthusiasm—as it is the case today in former Yugoslavia—with results in ethnic cleansing, mass slaughter and unending conflict that are horrible to contemplate.

The irony is that very often the former convert and the new believer are equally intolerant, equally dogmatic and violent. In recent years, alas, the swing from extreme Left to extreme Right has resulted in a tedious industry that pretends to independence and enlightenment but especially in the U.S. has only mirrored the ascendancy of Reaganism and Thatcherism. The American branch of this particular brand of self-promotion has called itself Second Thoughts, the idea being that first thoughts during the heady decade of the sixties were both radical and wrong. In a matter of months during the late 1980s Second Thoughts aspired to become a movement, alarmingly well funded by right-wing Maecenases like the Bradley and Olin Foundations. The specific impresarios were David Horowitz and Peter Collier, from whose pens a stream of books, one rather like the other, flowed, most of them the revelations of former radicals who had seen the light, and had become, in the words of one of them, vigorously pro-American and anticommunist.[2]

If sixties radicals, with their anti-Vietnam and anti-

---

[2]There is a shrewdly entertaining account of a Second Thoughts conference given by Christopher Hitchens, *For the Sake of Argument: Essays and Minority Reports* (London: Verso, 1993), pp. 111–14.

The fundamental problem is therefore how to reconcile one's identity and the actualities of one's own culture, society, and history to the reality of other identities, cultures, peoples. This can never be done simply by asserting one's preference for what is already one's own: tubthumping about the glories of "our" culture or the triumphs of "our" history is not worthy of the intellectual's energy, especially not today when so many societies are comprised of different races and backgrounds as to resist any reductive formulas. As I have tried to show here, the public realm in which intellectuals make their representations is extremely complex and contains uncomfortable features, but the meaning of an effective intervention in that realm has to rest on the intellectual's unbudgeable conviction in a concept of justice and fairness that allows for differences between nations and individuals, without at the same time assigning them to hidden hierarchies, preferences, evaluations. Everyone today professes a liberal language of equality and harmony for all. The problem for the intellectual is to bring these notions to bear on actual situations where the gap between the profession of equality and justice, on the one hand, and the rather less edifying reality, on the other, is very great.

This is most easily demonstrated in international relations, which is the reason I have stressed them so much in these lectures. A couple of recent examples illustrate what I have in mind. During the period just after Iraq's illegal invasion of Kuwait public discussion in the West justly focused on the unacceptability of the aggression which with extreme brutality sought to eliminate Kuwaiti as his own country, France, pursues similarly inhumane policies.[2]

It must be added, however, that Tocqueville (and John Stuart Mill for that matter, whose commendable ideas about democratic freedoms in England he said did not apply to India) lived during a period when the ideas of a universal norm of international behavior meant in effect the right of European power and European representations of other people to hold sway, so nugatory and secondary did the nonwhite peoples of the world seem. Besides, according to nineteenth-century Westerners, there were no independent African or Asian peoples of consequence to challenge the draconian brutality of laws that were applied unilaterally by colonial armies to black- or brown-skinned races. Their destiny was to be ruled. Frantz Fanon, Aimé Césaire, and C. L. R. James—to mention three great anti-imperialist black intellectuals—did not live and write until the twentieth century, so what they and the liberation movements of which they were a part accomplished culturally and politically in establishing the right of colonized peoples to equal treatment was not available to Tocqueville or Mill. But these changed perspectives are available to contemporary intellectuals who have not often drawn the inevitable conclusions, that if you wish to uphold basic human justice you must do so for everyone, not just selectively for the people that your side, your culture, your nation designates as okay.

[2] I have discussed the imperial context of this in detail in *Culture and Imperialism* (New York: Alfred A. Knopf, 1993), pp. 169–90.

Amerikan (*American* was always spelled with a 'k') polemics, were assertive and self-dramatizing in their beliefs, the Second Thoughters were equally loud and assertive. The only problem of course was that there was no Communist world now, no empire of evil, although there seemed to be no limit to the self-bowdlerizing and pious recitation of penitent formulas about the past that ensued. At bottom, though, it was the passage from one god to a new one that was really being celebrated. What had once been a movement based in part on enthusiastic idealism and dissatisfaction with the status quo was simplified and refashioned retrospectively by the Second Thoughters as little more than what they called abasement before the enemies of America and a criminal blindness to Communist brutality.[3]

In the Arab world, the brave, if airy and sometimes destructive, pan-Arab nationalism of the Nasser period which abated during the 1970s has been replaced with a set of local and regional creeds, most of them administered harshly by unpopular, uninspired minority regimes. They are now threatened by a whole array of Islamic movements. There has remained, however, a secular, cultural opposition in each Arab country; the most gifted writers, artists, political commentators, intellectuals, are generally a part of it, although they constitute a minority, many of whom have been hounded into silence or exile.

A more ominous phenomenon is the power and

[3]On the different varieties of self-disavowal a valuable text is E. P. Thompson's "Disenchantment or Apostasy? A Lay Sermon" in *Power and Consciousness,* ed. Conor Cruise O'Brien (New York: New York University Press, 1969), pp. 149–82.

wealth of the oil-rich states. A lot of the sensational Western media attention paid to the Baathi regimes of Syria
and Iraq has tended to overlook the quieter and insidious
pressure to conform exerted by governments who have a
lot of money to spend and offer academics, writers, and
artists munificent patronage. This pressure was particularly
in evidence during the Gulf crisis and war. Before the
crisis, Arabism had been supported and defended uncritically by progressive intellectuals who believed themselves
to be furthering the cause of Nasserism and the anti-
imperialist pro-independence impulse of the Bandung Conference and the nonaligned movement. In the immediate
aftermath of Iraq's occupation of Kuwait a dramatic re-
alignment of intellectuals took place. It has been suggested
that whole departments of the Egyptian publishing industry along with many journalists did an about-face. Former
Arab nationalists suddenly began to sing the praises of
Saudi Arabia and Kuwait, hated enemies of the past, new
friends and patrons now.

Lucrative rewards were probably offered to cause the
about-face to happen, but the Arab Second Thoughters
suddenly also discovered their passionate feelings about
Islam, as well as the singular virtues of one or another
ruling Gulf dynasty. Only a scant year or two before, many
of them (including Gulf regimes who subsidized Saddam
Hussein) sponsored paeans and festivals to Iraq as it fought
off Arabism's ancient foe, "the Persians." The language of
those earlier days was uncritical, bombastic, emotional, and
it reeked of hero-worship and quasi-religious effusion.
When Saudi Arabia invited George Bush and his armies

in, these voices were converted. This time they installed a formal, much-reiterated rejection of Arab nationalism (which they turned into a crude pastiche), fed by an uncritical support for the current rulers.

For Arab intellectuals matters have been further complicated by the new prominence of the U.S. as the major outside force in the Middle East today. What had once been an automatic and unthinking anti-Americanism—dogmatic, cliché-ridden, ludicrously simple—changed into pro-Americanism by fiat. In many newspapers and magazines throughout the Arab world, but especially those well known to be receiving the ever-handy Gulf subsidy, criticism of the United States was dramatically scaled-down, sometimes eliminated; this went along with the usual prohibitions against criticizing one or another regime, which was practically deified.

A very small handful of Arab intellectuals suddenly discovered a new role for themselves in Europe and the U.S. They had once been militant Marxists, often Trotskyists, and supporters of the Palestinian movement. After the Iranian revolution some had become Islamists. As the gods fled or were driven away, these intellectuals went mute, despite some calculated probing here and there as they searched for new gods to serve. One of them in particular, a man who had once been a loyal Trotskyist, later abandoned the Left and turned, as many others did, to the Gulf, where he made a handsome living in construction. He re-presented himself just before the Gulf crisis, and became an impassioned critic of one Arab regime in particular. He never wrote under his own name, but using a string of pseudonyms that protected his identity (and his interests) he flailed out indiscriminately and hysterically against Arab culture as a whole; he did this in such a way as to win him the attention of Western readers.

Now everyone knows that to try to say something in the mainstream Western media that is critical of U.S. policy or Israel is extremely difficult; conversely, to say things that are hostile to the Arabs as a people and culture, or Islam as a religion, is laughably easy. For in effect there is a cultural war between spokespersons for the West and those of the Muslim and Arab world. In so inflamed a situation, the hardest thing to do as an intellectual is to be critical, to refuse to adopt a rhetorical style that is the verbal equivalent of carpet-bombing, and to focus instead on those issues like U.S. support for unpopular client regimes, which for a person writing in the U.S. are somewhat more likely to be affected by critical discussion.

Of course, on the other hand, there is a virtual certainty of getting an audience if as an Arab intellectual you passionately, even slavishly support U.S. policy, you attack its critics, and if they happen to be Arabs, you invent evidence to show their villainy; if they are American you confect stories and situations that prove their duplicity; you spin out stories concerning Arabs and Muslims that have the effect of defaming their tradition, defacing their history, accentuating their weaknesses, of which of course there are plenty. Above all, you attack the officially approved enemies—Saddam Hussein, Baathism, Arab nationalism, the Palestinian movement, Arab views of Israel. And of course this earns you the expected accolades: you are characterized as courageous, you are outspoken and passionate, and on and on. The new god of course is the West. Arabs, you say, should try to be more like the West, should regard the West as a source and a reference point. Gone is the history of what the West actually did. Gone are the Gulf War's destructive results. We Arabs and Muslims are the sick ones, our problems are our own, totally self-inflicted.[4]

A number of things stand out about these kinds of performance. In the first place, there is no universalism here at all. Because you serve a god uncritically, all the devils are always on the other side: this was as true when you were a Trotskyist as it is now when you are a recanting former Trotskyist. You do not think of politics in terms of interrelationships or of common histories such as, for instance, the long and complicated dynamic that has bound the Arabs and Muslims to the West and vice versa. Real intellectual analysis forbids calling one side innocent, the other evil. Indeed the notion of a side is, where cultures are at issue, highly problematic, since most cultures aren't watertight little packages, all homogenous, and all either good or evil. But if your eye is on your patron, you cannot think as an intellectual, but only as a disciple or acolyte. In the back of your mind there is the thought that you must please and not displease.

In the second place, your own history of service to

<hr />

[4]A work that typifies some of these attitudes is Daryush Shayegan, *Cultural Schizophrenia: Islamic Societies Confronting the West*, trans. John Howe (London: Saqi Books, 1992).

previous masters is trampled on or demonized of course, but it doesn't provoke in you the slightest self-doubt, doesn't stimulate in you any desire to question the premise of loudly serving a god, then lurching impulsively to do the same for a new god. Far from it: as you had careened from one god to another in the past, you continue to do the same thing in the present, a bit more cynically it is true, but in the end with the same effect.

By contrast the true intellectual is a secular being. However much intellectuals pretend that their representations are of higher things or ultimate values, morality begins with their activity in this secular world of ours—where it takes place, whose interests it serves, how it jibes with a consistent and universalist ethic, how it discriminates between power and justice, what it reveals of one's choices and priorities. Those gods that always fail demand from the intellectual in the end a kind of absolute certainty and a total, seamless view of reality that recognizes only disciples or enemies.

What strikes me as much more interesting is how to keep a space in the mind open for doubt and for the part of an alert, skeptical irony (preferably also self-irony). Yes, you have convictions and you make judgments, but they are arrived at by work, and by a sense of association with others, other intellectuals, a grassroots movement, a continuing history, a set of lived lives. As for abstractions or orthodoxies, the trouble with them is that they are patrons who need placating and stroking all the time. The morality and principles of an intellectual should not constitute a sort of sealed gearbox that drives thought and action in one direction and is powered by an engine with only one fuel source. The intellectual has to walk around, has to have the space in which to stand and talk back to authority, since unquestioning subservience to authority in today's world is one of the greatest threats to an active, and moral, intellectual life.

It is difficult to face that threat on one's own, and even more difficult to find a way to be consistent with your beliefs and at the same time remain free enough to grow, change your mind, discover new things, or rediscover what you had once put aside. The hardest aspect of being an intellectual is to represent what you profess through your work and interventions, without hardening into an institution or a kind of automaton acting at the behest of a system or method. Anyone who has felt the exhilaration of being successful at that *and* also successful at keeping alert and solid will appreciate how rare the convergence is. But the only way of ever achieving it is to keep reminding yourself that as an intellectual you are the one who can choose between actively representing the truth to the best of your ability and passively allowing a patron or an authority to direct you. For the secular intellectual, *those* gods always fail.

Also by EDWARD W. SAID

The Politics of Dispossession:
The Struggle for Palestinian Self-Determination, 1969–1994

In this stunning collection of essays, Edward Said traces his people's struggle for statehood through twenty-five years of exile, from the PLO's bloody 1970 exile from Jordan to the ambiguous 1994 peace accord with Israel.

History/Middle Eastern Studies/0-679-76145-4

Culture and Imperialism

Culture and Imperialism offers a powerful investigation of the relationship between the Western imperial endeavor and the culture that both reflected and reinforced it. Probing masterpieces of the Western tradition, Said shows how the justification for empire-building in the nineteenth and early twentieth centuries was inescapably embedded in the cultural imagination of the West.

History/Cultural Criticism/0-679-75054-1

Orientalism

In this brilliant work of intellectual history, updated with a new afterword, Said explores the themes of Orientalism, as subject, as representation, and as institution. It is "intellectual history on a high order . . . and very exciting" (*The New York Times*).

Near Eastern Studies/Cultural History/0-394-74067-X

The Question of Palestine

Updated with a new preface and epilogue, this pioneering work encompasses the most recent developments in the Middle East and shows how events large and small during the past several years have affected the chances for an independent Palestine.

Current Affairs/History/0-679-73988-2

Available at your local bookstore,
or call toll-free to order: 1-800-793-2665 (credit cards only).